SIMPLY SEAWEED

Lesley Ellis

GRUB STREET · LONDON

Dedicated to
Ron, Oliver and Maddy

Published by Grub Street
The Basement, 10 Chivalry Road, London SW11 1HT

Copyright © Grub Street 1998
Text copyright © Lesley Ellis 1998

British Library Cataloguing in Publication Data
Ellis, Lesley
Simply Seaweed
I. Title
641.8
ISBN 1 898697 45 0

Printed and bound in Italy by Vallardi

Acknowledgements

I would like to thank the following people and organisations for their kind help in preparing this book: the staff of Buckinghamshire county libraries; Carabay Seaweeds, Galway; Clearspring Ltd, London (and especially Frances Toase); Steve Downey of Heritage Fine Foods, Bristol; Maine Coast Sea Vegetables, Maine, USA; the Norwegian Trade Council; Paul Sellars of the Pig 'n' Fish, St Ives, Cornwall; Pronova Biopolymer, Drammen, Norway; Ian Tittley of the Natural History Museum, London; Wessex Food Brokers; and especially Ron, Oliver and Maddy for enthusiastically testing and tasting any number of different seaweed dishes and to my mother, Davette Spong, for her enthusiasm in our seaweed-gathering ventures.

Bibliography

The Best of British Fish and Seafood, Ellis, L (Dial House, 1995); *The Book of Seaweed*, Major, A (Gordon & Cremonesi,1977); *British Seaweed*, Dickinson, C I (Eyre & Spottiswoode, 1963); *Cooking With Sea Vegetables*, Bradford, P & M (Thorsons, 1985) *English Food*, Grigson, J (Macmillan 1974); *The Fish Book*, Perrin, K (Chatto & Windus, 1989); *Floyd on Britain & Ireland*, Floyd, K (BBC Books, 1989); *Food for Free*, Mabey, R (HarperCollins, 1992); *Food in England*, Hartley, D (McDonald & Janes, 1978); *Food Lovers' Guide to Britain*, Green, H (BBC Books, 1995); *The Food of the Western World*, FitzGibbon, T (Hutchinson & Co , 1976); *In Search of Food*, Mabey, D (McDonald & Janes, 1978); *Introducing Macrobiotic Cooking*, Eski, W (Japan Publications Inc, 1978); *Japanese Cookery*, Spayde, J (Century, 1984); *Larousse Gastronomique*, ed Froud, N & Turgeon, C (Paul Hamlyn, 1965); *The Laverbread Cookbook* (Wales Tourist Board); *The Little Hebridean Pot-boiler* (Cleadale Crafts, 1990); *Maine Coast Sea Vegetable Recipes* (Maine Coast Sea Vegetables); *North Atlantic Seafood* Davidson, A (Penguin, 1980, reprinted 1986); *Oriental Cookery Course* ed. Powling, S (Hamlyn, 1990); *Plants that Feed and Serve Us*, Hvass, E (Blandford Press, 1973); *The Sea Vegetable Book*, Madlener, J C (C N Potter Inc, 1977); *Seaweed*, Surrey-Gent, S (*Outdoors Illustrated*, Oct-Nov 1995); *The Seaweed Server*, Guiry, M (World Wide Web, January 1996); *Seaweeds and their Uses*, Chapman VJ & DJ (Chapman & Hall, 1980); *The World Atlas of Food* (Mitchell Beazley, 1975).

Contents

Introduction

You only have to mention eating seaweed and it conjures up images of exotic or Oriental cuisine for most of us, but seaweed dishes are nothing new or trendy or foreign. Traditional western recipes include: ocean-flavoured Welsh laverbread, oatmeal-rolled and fried up into crispy little breakfast cakes; delicate Irish carragheen puddings and savoury Icelandic fish dishes seasoned with tangy black snippets of dulse.

So why is it that most of us would be hard-pressed to name even one variety of local seaweed, let alone know how to whip up a delicious dish with it? The truth is that although seaweed has been eaten in Europe and America for many hundreds of years, it has always played something of a minor role in people's diets, as tasty flavourings, crunchy garnishes, salads and relishes to give interest and sparkle to everyday food.

Historically our taste for seaweed (along with many other wild plants) took a down-turn, probably at the time of the Industrial Revolution when a cornucopia of manufactured foodstuffs were suddenly on offer to ordinary folk. Presumably locally-gathered seaweed started to seem rather tame in the face of all that seductive packaging and colour printing.

Now, happily, things are beginning to change and native seaweed seems set to make something of a comeback, as food enthusiasts and restaurateurs become more adventurous with ingredients, keen to explore new tastes and texture, and curious about our neglected food traditions and heritage.

Carabay Seaweeds in Galway, Ireland (possibly the largest seaweed producer in Ireland and Britain) is one firm that is confident about the future of seaweed and is planning for growth, investing in new drying equipment, conducting surveys of the coast for new harvestable beds and looking at new "traditional" species such as sea lettuce (*Ulva lactuca*) and dabberlocks (*Alaria esculenta*) to add to their product range.

Not that traditional seaweed ever was altogether abandoned – there are places around Britain, Ireland, Europe and North America where people have happily carried on harvesting and enjoying their native seaweed just as they always did, albeit on a modest scale. Cardiff, in South Wales, is a good example.

It is in the heart of Cardiff at the entrance to the old city market hall that you will find Ashton's the fishmonger. Make your way to the counter and you will see among the ice-sprinkled pyramids of fish a great tub of glistening black-green purée. This is laverbread; it is made from boiled *Porphyra umbilicalis*, or laver seaweed and it is a great Welsh speciality. You can buy it by the quarter-pound (125g) to roll with oatmeal into little cakes and fry to a crisp with eggs, bacon and cockles for a rib-sticking Welsh breakfast. Local restaurants serve it too, especially with seafood. Laver seaweed can be found clinging to exposed rocks all around the British coast. The Welsh coal miners used to be great laver eaters, and South Wales is the stronghold of the British laver trade, though by no means as great as it once was – Penclawwd on the Gower Peninsula is the remaining centre of the industry. Scottish fishing communities used to eat quite a lot of laver, too; they called it slouk and made it into a jelly to eat with oatcakes, but they don't bother with it much now, and send supplies south to supplement Welsh demand. In Ireland it is called sloke.

You can track laver down elsewhere with a bit of detective work – try Butcher's Row in Barnstaple, Devon, a quaint old street which used to boast 42 butchers shops. One of the few survivors, Massey's, sells locally gathered laver.

Dulse which is usually called dillisk (*dilleasc* in Gaelic) or *creathnach* in Ireland is a popular readily-available commodity. Dulse is sold dried as a chewy salty snack. You will find it for sale, along with yellowman toffee, at traditional fairs. And it is also cooked into all kinds of potato dishes – dulse has a great affinity with potato.

Carragheen, which got its name from the Irish village which once had a thriving industry in the seaweed, is also quite easily come by in Ireland. Sometimes called Irish moss, it is used for its gelling properties and is boiled up in milk or water to make jellies and blancmanges.

Dulse and carragheen are also sometimes still harvested along the west coast of Scotland and in the Orkneys and the Hebrides. Alan Major in his *Book of Seaweed* quotes an old Scottish saying "He who eats of the dulse of Guerdie and drinks of the wells of Kildingie will escape all maladies except the Black Death." (Presumably, nutrient-rich dulse provided a useful food supplement to boost flagging immune systems in the days before the multi-vitamin capsule.) As for carragheen, I bought excellent supplies on the Isle of Eigg a couple of years ago, but the stuff I use now, which I get from Mr Oates our West Indian grocer, comes from Ireland. It is also good, but rather more bleached than the pretty pink and purple Hebridean version.

Samphire is different from other species, in that it isn't really a seaweed at all but a seashore plant. Well-known in Elizabethan England, this succulent vegetable is now making something of a comeback. You will find it these days in many fishmongers in the summer and as a fashionable addition to restaurant menus. Quite rightly, in my opinion, for it's a delicious crunchy vegetable or garnish for fish and seafood. Samphire was eaten by many 400 years ago – in Shakespeare's *King Lear*, one of the characters peers over a horrid great cliff and exclaims "Half-way down hangs one who gathers samphire - dreadful trade!" This poor precarious samphire picker was probably collecting rock samphire, as opposed to marsh samphire which is the shore plant that is eaten today.

Britain and Ireland are not alone in Europe for having seaweed-eating traditions of course. Dulse was used in Norway in times gone by, and in Iceland where it was eaten with dried fish, butter and potatoes. Alan Davidson in his book *North Atlantic Seafood* gives an Icelandic recipe for haddock sprinkled with dulse, as a salty garnish. On the Kamchatka Peninsula dulse has also been used for brewing – maybe for want of other raw materials.

Dulse is also gathered along the Mediterranean coast, especially in France. In Brittany it is traditionally mixed with the kelp known as oarweed (in Japan called sweet kombu) and boiled into a kind of jelly called *pain d'algues*.

Dabberlocks or *Alaria esculenta* is another seaweed traditionally gathered and eaten in Europe. In Ireland it is known as murlin, in Scotland as henware. It has also been eaten in Iceland and the Faeroe Islands. I don't think you will find dabberlocks for sale anywhere in Britain or Ireland at the present time (it may be harvested in Galway in the near future), but go to the eastern seaboard of North America, and you will discover a small but thriving industry harvesting, drying and selling it. In fact, the Bay of Fundy on the border of Canada and northern USA must be one of the most important sources of edible seaweed in the West, yielding thousands of dollars worth of seaweed each year – not only dabberlocks but laver, kelps, and especially dulse. Some of the Bay of Fundy dulse even finds its way to Britain; and very delicate and good it is too.

It was 19th-century Irish and Scottish immigrants who first brought an enthusiasm for dulse and carragheen to the eastern states of North America. Today, in maritime provinces of Canada and New England, dried dulse is still popular, used as a relish, simply chewed (a bit like chewing tobacco) or finely snipped over savoury dishes. Carragheen, a regular item in 19th-century Irish households for making jellies, is still harvested in the region to make refined carrageenan, a gelling agent for the food industry, used in ice-creams, desserts, jellies and blancmanges.

China somehow seems far more likely to be a seaweed producer than America but in fact this is not the case. Native Americans on both sides of the continent have their own traditions of collecting and eating seaweed – dabberlocks (*alaria*), kelp and laver. Although when Chinese settlers first arrived in California, they didn't use local supplies of laver (their favourite seaweed) but imported what they needed from China, after a time a local laver industry developed and by 1929, the seaweed was being shipped back in the other direction to China.

Of course, the Chinese, like every other immigrant group, brought with them to the west their own distinctive cuisines. Today, Far Eastern cuisines – Chinese, Japanese, Thai, Indonesian – are all hugely popular and the ethnic restaurant trade is flourishing. In fact, it is probably true to say that many westerners get their first taste of seaweed sitting in a Japanese restaurant. You can hardly eat a Japanese meal without coming across seaweed in some form or other: delicately garnishing raw slices of fish; shinily wrapping little bundles of vinegared rice or floating in green squares on top of a bowl of chicken broth.

Certainly Japanese seaweed varieties are the ones that are making their way into our major supermarket chains at present, along with soy sauce and rice crackers as part of specialist Japanese food ranges. And it is Japanese seaweed that is mainly bought and eaten by western macrobiotics and healthfood enthusiasts.

The Japanese are the world's most dedicated seaweed eaters. Everyone in Japan eats it and over 20 different species are commonly consumed – the most important kinds being the different varieties of kelp (kombu), laver (nori), wakame, arame, hijiki and the various seaweed species used for producing agar (kanten) for jelly-making. According to one recent source, the Japanese consume an astonishing 9,000,000,000 sheets of nori, alone, every year. In Japan, seaweed is not just gathered from the wild; the coastal waters are also intensively farmed for species such as nori and wakame.

Other Far Eastern countries that eat seaweed include Korea which harvests thousands of tonnes of wakame each year, the Philippines, Indonesia, Vietnam and Burma. Many countries in eastern Asia also boil up local seaweed to produce agar for making an array of blancmanges and jellies. *Woon waan* is a favourite Thai dessert – little brightly coloured agar jelly moulds, very sweet, which can be served with thickened coconut milk, while *Thach* is a typical Vietnamese jelly.

The Chinese also make agar puddings as well as using seaweed in savoury dishes. Don't be misled by that famous Chinese dish 'Crispy Seaweed', however, which isn't seaweed at all but finely shredded cabbage deep-fried until it is turns dark green, curled and shiny and looks remarkably like the real stuff. If you are looking for real Chinese seaweed, laver (Japanese nori) and kelp (kombu) are the most common kinds in Chinese supermarkets in Britain.

It is not just the Asians who are great seaweed eaters – the Hawaiians are also enthusiasts who have harvested and eaten local varieties for hundreds of years – luxuriant masses of both red and green seaweed, or "limu" flourish in their lagoons and coral pools. The Maoris also used to eat various seaweed varieties in soups and salads, and use a kind of laver, while the Australian aborigines traditionally used one or two types of seaweed, which they would dry and roast for storing, then soak before eating.

In the West Indies jellies are prepared from local seaweed, although West Indian communities in Britain now use carragheen as a substitute ingredient in recipes such as Jamaican Sea Moss (on page 84).

Seaweed harvesting today is by no means a folksy local phenomenon. It's big business. Outside Japan, most seaweed gets used, not directly as food, but as raw material for industry. Products range from fertilisers and seaweed meal for livestock feed, to the alginates which are used by the food industry as stabilisers and emulsifiers in an astonishing variety of products. It is quite likely that seaweed went into making the ice cream in your freezer not to mention the foam on the top of your pint and even the jelly in the dog's food.

Another recent growth area for seaweed is production of vitamin supplements and food supplements. Seaweed is packed with nutrients, a quality that healthfood manufacturers are now keen to exploit commercially.

The world's seaweeds, properly managed, offer a massive renewable resource and it seems that industrial uses can only grow. But alongside the giant industries, it's good to know that there are the small independent companies which harvest seaweed on a modest scale as food for the cook and the gourmet, in response to a growing enthusiasm for traditional wild foods and flavours.

A Cook's Guide to Seaweed

AGAR Kanten (Japan)

Agar is used for making jellies and aspics. It is usually sold in packets
of flakes; in Japan you will also find it sold in strands and solid blocks
or bars. Powdered agar, made by chemically extracting the gel from
the seaweed, is considered to be inferior to the flakes which are made
by the traditional method. This involves boiling seaweed (various
species are used), then leaving the jelly liquor to freeze-dry in the
snow for a fortnight, a technique taught to the Japanese by the
Chinese in the 17th century, and still used today.

Agar produces a neutral-tasting jelly. It takes a little longer to melt
than gelatine (sprinkle it into already simmering water and stir for 3-4
minutes) but sets more quickly, to a firm, smooth, silky texture. It is
an ideal gelling agent for vegetarians and is good for blancmanges,
snows (Apple Snow, page 83), jellies and aspics. It is also the perfect
gelling agent for warm climates, because it stays firm even in hot
weather and over-heated rooms, which is probably why it is the
traditional gelling agent for so many Far Eastern jellies, sweets and
desserts (Apple Kanten, page 81, Almond Custard, page 82).

ALARIA *Alaria esculenta*

Dabberlocks, bladderlocks, henware (Scotland) murlin (Ireland),
winged kelp or alaria (USA). Japanese alaria is very closely related.

The long yellowish-olive coloured fronds of this seaweed flourish near
the low water mark on the exposed shores of cold northern oceans.
The juicy midribs of young plants are traditionally eaten in parts of
Scotland and Ireland, and are described by one author as tasting a bit
like radish tops.

Dried alaria is not, as far as I know, available in Britain, but it may
soon be sold by a firm in Galway. It is harvested from the eastern
seaboard of America, dried and sold in healthfood shops and by mail
order. It is excellent in soups and very good as a wrapping for fish or
savoury fillings. It can also be chopped into salads, after soaking or
marinating for about 20 minutes. If you cannot get hold of alaria, use
dried Japanese wakame instead – a related and very similar species.
Alaria needs cooking for a good 20 minutes to become very tender.
It has a mild, sweet flavour.

ARAME *Eisenia bicyclis*

This is a mild-tasting Japanese seaweed. It is harvested from the Pacific coastline of Japan, especially around the Ise peninsula. Traditionally, women divers picked the arame leaves from below the water-line where it grows. Once harvested, the seaweed is boiled for several hours, then shredded and dried, which is how you buy it in packets. The black strands turn dark brown when soaked for a few minutes. They don't need much cooking.

Use arame in stir-fries (Stir-Fried Vegetables with Arame, page 68), salads (Arame California Salad, page 63; Mediterranean Salad with Arame Dressing, page 60), stews, with noodles, pasta, rice and vegetable dishes (Savoury Rice with Arame, page 46), adding it about 3 minutes before the end of the cooking time. In Japan it is especially used in soups or boiled then eaten with soy sauce – when it is not being hung up as a popular New Year decoration.

Don't confuse arame with hijiki, which looks similar. Arame has a gentler, sweeter taste and smoother, softer texture.

CARRAGHEEN *Chondrus crispus*
Irish moss, Dorset moss, Iberian moss

This, to me, is the prettiest of all the edible seaweeds – a fan of delicate frilly pink, purple and cream fronds. After gathering clumps of the weed along the mid-tideline rocks (mainly in the summer months), the carragheen harvester washes the seaweed thoroughly, then spreads it out in the open air to dry. During this time it bleaches from purple-red through pink to cream. The creamier coloured your dried carragheen looks, the less flavour it will have, and less goodness.

Traditionally, carragheen has been used in Scotland, Ireland, Yorkshire, and along the east coast of North America. It was also at one time sold as an invalid food under the name of Iberian moss. It is still harvested in Ireland and North America, and on a very small scale in the Scottish islands.

Carragheen is used as a gelling agent, boiled into milk jellies and puddings (Irish Moss Ginger Pudding, page 79; Irish Moss Pudding. with Rich Whiskey Sauce, page 80; Carragheen Mould, page 78), for thickening soups and stews and in a traditional Jamaican recipe, for a thick spiced milk shake (Jamaican Sea Moss, page 84). It was also at one time boiled with hot milk and honey to make a soothing drink for coughs and colds, and recommended for stomach complaints and sleeplessness. Carragheen has a pleasant, distinctive ocean flavour.

You may not like this taste in pudding but used as an aspic for seafood, the marine flavour works very well (Prawns a Carragheen Aspic, page 49). Like agar, carragheen is a good vegetarian substitute for gelatine.

Carragheen should be washed under running water and picked over before use. Fresh carragheen should be washed in several changes of water. You will need 10-15 g (¼-½ oz) dried carragheen boiled in 900 ml (1½ pt) to set to a jelly, depending on how firm a set you want. Boil for up to 1 hour until the liquid thickens, then strain it off and discard the seaweed. It seems to me that some batches of carragheen set more easily than others, so adjust the quantity of seaweed and cooking time according to your particular supply.

Some pudding recipes suggest you rub the well-boiled carragheen through a sieve rather than strain it out and this gives a speckled-oatmeal appearance to the pudding, a firmer set and a more pronounced flavour.

DULSE *Palmaria (Rhodymenia) Palmata*
Dillisk/*Dilleasc*/*Creathnach* (Ireland)

Traditionally harvested and eaten in Ireland, Scotland, Iceland, Greenland, Norway, France, the Faeroe Islands, eastern Siberia, and along the eastern seaboard of New England and Canada, dulse is probably the most commonly eaten of the North Atlantic seaweeds. It is still produced in Ireland, in the Bay of Fundy and along the shores of Nova Scotia in North America, and in France.

Dulse grows along the low water-line on rocky exposed shores, small plants about 15-30 cm (6-12") high with maroon-coloured, leathery fronds, which are usually hand-picked, then wind-and sun-dried. It is sold dried in packets, as dark-red pliable bundles of flat leaves. However Tesco and Waitrose supermarkets sell punnets of fresh dulse, which just needs rinsing in cold water for 2-3 minutes before cooking.

The dried American dulse I buy is very tender and cooks in 5-6 minutes, but supplies vary and you may have to soak and cook yours for longer. The salty, piquant flavour of dulse makes a good relish. Roll up a bundle of the dried leaves then snip fragments off the end with scissors to sprinkle over fish dishes. Alternatively, soak the leaves (boil if necessary), then add them to sauces (Lasagne with Dulse, page 54) and mayonnaises or soups.

Dulse combines well with butter, and also with potatoes: in Hebridean Dulse Broth for example, (page 25); and in traditional

Icelandic dishes with fish and potatoes (Salt Cod and Dulse, page 47). The slightly spicy marine flavour marries well with fish and seafood: Icelandic Haddock with Dulse, page 42; Fresh Noodles made with Seaweed, page 70. Be wary how you season dishes containing dulse, which can be quite salty.

In Ireland and eastern North America, dried dulse is munched as a chewy snack; Michael Guiry of University College, Galway, says it goes well with dark ales and stouts.

Dulse is a rich source of protein and vitamins, including vitamin C. Dorothy Hartley, in *Food in England*, says that she found dulse most popular in places near the sites of old whaling stations. The famous French chef Soyer recommended dulse be added to his St Patrick's soup, which he devised to be fed to victims of the Irish famine in 1847.

Pepper dulse (*Laurencia pinnatifida*) is a separate species, which looks similar to proper dulse but has a stronger, peppery flavour and is traditionally used as a condiment.

HIJIKI *Hijikia fusiforme*

This glossy black, richly flavoured seaweed is eaten in Japan, China and Korea. It grows on rocks near the low-water mark and is collected early in the year when the plants are young and tender. You will find it sold shredded and dried in packets.

Soak the hijiki for about 10 minutes before cooking and simmer for about 30 minutes until it is tender – it will swell 3-5 times its size. Then add it to stir-fries, salads and vegetable dishes.

Hijiki combines well with sweet ingredients. Try cooking it in apple juice with a dash of soy sauce to mellow and round the flavour (Hijiki Salad, page 59). Sweet sherry, or sweet rice wine are good additions to marinades and salad dressings. Hijiki is excellent in hot, spicy dishes (Spicy Chicken and Hijiki Pancakes, page 38) and combines well with oily foods. It is good with sweet and sour dishes, and rich curries.

KELP *Laminaria spp*

The kelps are large brown seaweeds which grow together in thick sub-marine forests. Several members of the kelp family are important as food.

Laminaria digitata
Kelp, Tangle, Local kombu (Britain), Horsetail kelp (USA)

This Atlantic kelp has broad fronds, the ends of which split with age into broad ribbons, which make it look a bit like a hand. You will find it mainly sold in packets of 13cm (5") dried strips. Cook it and use it in all the same ways as its near relative, Japanese kelp (kombu) (see below). The two species are very similar, but perhaps the local kelp has a little more texture and flavour.

Tangle fronds were at one time boiled up as vegetable and served with butter in the Hebrides.

Laminaria japonica
Kombu, Japanese kelp (Britain, USA), Royal kombu (Japan, Korea)

Kelp is one of the most important seaweeds in Japanese cuisine. Various different species are used in Japan, but this is the one you will probably come across. It is one of the sweeter varieties, used for making sweetmeats in Japan, but just as good in savoury recipes.

It is usually sold in dried sheets, or packets of strips about 13cm (5") long. The white bloom on the strips are mineral salts.

In Japan, one of the most important uses of kelp (kombu) is in making stock for sauces (Crispy Seaweed Tempura, page 31) and soups (Japanese Chicken Soup, page 28)

The classic Japanese stock, dashi is made from kelp and dried bonito flakes (katsuo-bushi – available from Japanese grocers). A properly made dashi is essential if you are going to cook truly authentic Japanese food.

DASHI (Japanese stock): Put 1.2 litre (2 pt) water in a saucepan; add 25 g (1 oz) Japanese kelp and heat. Just before the water boils, remove the kelp and add 25 g (1 oz) bonito flakes. Bring the water rapidly to a boil for 2-3 seconds – no more – then remove from the heat and strain immediately. Alternatively, you can buy instant sachets from Japanese food shops.

For a more general-purpose stock, put a piece of kombu in a saucepan of water and boil for about 20 minutes, then remove before adding soy sauce and perhaps a squeeze of ginger juice. Japanese kelp is also good cooked with beans; it adds flavour, reduces the cooking time and helps to make the beans more digestible (apparently, because of the glutamic acid it contains which is a natural tenderiser). Just drain your dried beans that have been soaking overnight, place them in a saucepan covered with water, add a piece of kombu and cook as usual until the beans are tender.

Kelp is also good finely slivered and fried into crisps, with or without batter (Crispy Seaweed Tempura, page 31), or used as a bed for cooking fish or vegetables (Sea Bream Steamed on Seaweed, page 44) and it is good made into a pickle (Pickled Kelp, page 73)

Laminaria longicruris
Kelp, Atlantic kombu (USA)

This is a kind of kelp which is harvested off the east coast of North America. It is sold dried in packets in the USA and Canada, and can be used in all the same ways as the thinner Japanese kelp (kombu), but cooks rather more quickly – if left to boil in liquid for more than 20 minutes it will dissolve altogether.

Laminaria saccharina
Oarweed, Sea belt, Sugar wrack, Poor man's weatherglass, Sweet kelp, Sweet kombu (Britain), Sugar kelp, Tangleweed (North America)

This is the seaweed people hang up to foretell the weather – it goes floppy as humidity increases (possibly foreboding rain) and dry and hard as the air dries. Its hugely long, frilly-edged brown fronds can grow to 10m(30ft). Traditionally Hebridean children chewed the sweet stalks as "sweeties" which apparently taste a bit like peanuts.

Mannitol, a kind of sugar, is produced as a white powdery substance on the fronds of this seaweed when it is dried. Industry uses this in various ways, including as a dusting powder on chewing gum.

Sweet kelp can be used in all the same ways as other kelps – this naturally sweet kind is ideal for candying and making Japanese sweetmeats.

KELP POWDER
You may well come across packets of this in healthfood stores. Sold mainly as a food supplement, it is quite strongly flavoured, but can be used as a seasoning for soups and other savoury dishes. Seagreens Culinary Granuals are available too, for use in home baked bread and pizza dough, or for sprinkling on fish before baking, rice dishes, potatoes, fish cakes, pasta or even salads. It gives a nutty, ocean taste.

LAVER Porphyra spp
Bara lawr/Laverbread (Wales), Purple laver, Black butter (England),

Slouk (Scotland), Sloke (Ireland), Nori (Japan)

Various species of this little thin-leafed, red seaweed are used throughout the world. The Maoris use a kind they call *karengo*, while native Americans in Alaska, Canada and the USA eat other types, including a variety known as "fluted nori". The Chinese, and Koreans are also great laver eaters. The laver I have come across in Chinese supermarkets is sold in dried bundles of large flat sheets, dark green and quite salty, although I understand that the wild laver that is harvested off the east coast of North America is dried and sold in packets of small whole plants.

The Japanese are the world's biggest consumers of laver. You are most likely to come across it in thin dried sheets, either shiny black (nori) or shiny green (sushi nori), the difference being that the sushi nori has already been toasted. Most Japanese recipes recommend that nori is toasted before use – and even the sushi nori benefits from a quick toast to freshen up the flavour.

TOASTING NORI

To toast a sheet of nori, pass it swiftly backwards and forwards over a flame two or three times until it turns from black to green.

Nori sheets are excellent for wrapping around fish, rice, and savoury mixtures (Savoury Stuffed Seaweed Parcels, page 57). In Japan, nori is classically used as a wrapping material for sushi, or vinegared rice (Sushi Rolls, page 34), and shredded as a garnish.

Green nori flakes (*ao nori*) are sold in packets and boxes for shaking over soups, noodles, rice, salads and other dishes as a seasoning (Japanese Noodles with Seaweed, page 69; Nori-Coated Savoury Nuts, page 33). They have a pleasant, mild savoury taste. The flakes are made from a type of seaweed which is not, in fact, a true member of the laver family. Real laver, however, makes a good substitute if you can't get hold of the flakes – simply toast a sheet of nori, then shred it very finely.

In South Wales and parts of the south coast of England, laver is boiled to a purée called laverbread, and sold ready-cooked by the quarter-pound in markets, fishmongers, butchers and healthfood stores. It is also canned by a firm in South Wales and available by mail order and in specialist food halls. Laver purée keeps very well for 2 or 3 months in the freezer, and can be defrosted and used just the same as the fresh purée.

In Wales, laver purée is made into little oatmeal-coated cakes and fried for breakfast (Laverbread, page 65). It is also traditionally used to make an excellent sauce for mutton or seafood (Roast Lamb with Rosemary and Laver Sauce, page 37, Stuffed Sewin with Laver Sauce, page 51).

Another classic way to eat laver purée is to mix it with olive oil and lemon juice, season it carefully, then use it as a pâté on toast or oatcakes. It can also be used in virtually all the same ways that you would use spinach purée – for making green pasta (Fresh Noodles made with Seaweed page 70), stirring into sauces, and mixing into cheese dishes and quiches. The subtle, oceany flavour of laver combines particularly well with seafood, butter and lemon juice.

For most Welsh and English laver recipes, you need laver purée. If you can't get this fresh, frozen or canned, dried Japanese nori cooked to a purée will make an acceptable substitute. Here's how:

LAVER PURÉE FROM DRIED NORI SHEETS: Untoasted nori sheets are best; allow 15 g (½ oz) dried nori to make 125 g (4 oz) laver purée. Tear up the nori and put it in a saucepan with about 300 ml (½ pt) water. Bring to the boil, then simmer for about 5 minutes, stirring, until the nori disintegrates completely. Drain off any remaining water, and you should be left with about 125 g (4 oz). For a dry purée (to make Fresh Noodles made with Seaweed, page 70 for example) pour the purée into a fine sieve and leave it to drain for about 5 minutes, until you are left with about 50 g (2 oz).

SAMPHIRE Salicornia spp

Marsh samphire grows in muddy estuaries and salt marshes, a stumpy, bushy plant with succulent knobby stems and leaves.
It is also called glasswort because it was at one time used in the manufacture of glassware. It isn't actually a seaweed but a seashore plant. It has a salty marine taste, a crunchy succulent texture and certainly deserves to be included in any discussion on sea vegetables. This and the unrelated rock samphire (see below) have been eaten in Britain for centuries.

Marsh samphire has become tremendously popular in the last couple years and suppliers can scarcely keep up with demand from restaurants. It is available in Britain from fishmongers and markets during the short season of June or July to August. Steve Downey of Heritage Fine Foods, who supplies some of Britain's top chefs, extends the brief season by bringing samphire from as far as Saudi

Arabia in February and March, then moving on to French sources for the spring, and finishing with English supplies in the summer.

Steve Downey also supplies French pickled samphire, sold in 1 kg (2lb) jars. Not as good as fresh, of course, although I have heard that some restaurants are not above washing the pickled product, steaming it for a few minutes, then serving it as a vegetable to diners eager for samphire in the winter months. Pickled samphire is excellent for garnishes, dressings, salads and anywhere you would use a pickled vegetable.

Fresh samphire is best prepared and served as simply as possible. Wash it, pick over the plant and remove any discoloured leaves and woody stems. Tender young pieces are good eaten raw in salads, or used as a crisp, bright garnish to seafood and fish dishes.

It is also good cooked: steam it for about 6-8 minutes, or boil rapidly for 2-5 minutes in lots of unsalted water, testing regularly to make sure you don't overcook it. Then serve it with a big knob of butter or a butter sauce (Samphire with Nut-Brown Butter Sauce, page 64)

Alternatively, you can stuff samphire into the cavity of any fish you are going to bake. Just dot with unsalted butter, and moisten with a couple of tablespoons of white wine. Or try it broken up into seafood stir-fries or risottos, or whizzed in a food processor with butter to make a beautiful green sauce. It's great with whiting – its wonderful ocean flavour will help along the gentle flavour of the fish. It is also a traditional accompaniment to mutton.

Samphire can be extremely salty. Do not add salt to cooking water, use unsalted butter with it and taste before you season any dish containing samphire.

Rock samphire (*Crithmum maritimum*) which has a distinctive almost sulphurous smell, was often pickled in days gone by. One 17th-century recipe, quoted by Theodora FitzGibbon in *The Food of the Western World*, combines rock samphire with pickled cucumbers, capers, vinegar, lemon, salt and nutmeg, strong broth and sugar, thickened with butter and egg yolk.

SEA LETTUCE *Ulva spp*

Various species of this delicate-leafed, green seaweed are used in the Far East, Chile and the West Indies, cooked in soups and eaten raw in salads. In parts of China it is used as a medicine against fevers.

Sometimes known as green laver, sea lettuce is not a member of the laver (*Porphyra*) seaweeds, but can be cooked into a purée in much the same way though some people say it is inferior to real laver.

Tesco and Waitrose sell fresh sea lettuce. It comes in 100g punnets and just needs rinsing before use.

A word of warning if you are gathering your own – sea lettuce tends to proliferate in sewage outfall areas – not the sort of waters you will want to harvest, so be extra careful when picking this species.

WAKAME *Undaria spp*

This pretty, green, frilly-fronded seaweed is popular in Japan (where it is farmed) and Korea. You will probably find it sold in dried strips which are an uninspiring dusty-grey colour. Soak them in water to watch the transformation back to verdant leafiness.

Wakame is used raw in salads, cooked in soups and baked. It is excellent for wrapping around fish to keep it moist as it cooks, or for making savoury parcels (Wakame Wrapped Sardines, page 48). If you are using it as a wrapping material, soak it, then remove the thick midrib first.

Soak wakame for about 10 minutes, then it can be boiled for 20 minutes to make it very tender. Once cooked it has a very soft texture and a mild, sweet flavour. Wakame is a good substitute for alaria.

THE RECIPES

Vegans and vegetarians

If you are vegan or on a non-dairy diet, you will want to use substitutes for dairy products in the meatless recipes included here. Non-dairy alternatives will work perfectly well in these recipes – use a good quality oil or non-dairy margarine for shallow frying (not a low-fat variety) and substitute soya milk for cow's milk. Heat soya milk very carefully to prevent it burning on the bottom of the pan. You may find you need some extra sugar in puddings made with unsweetened soya milk. I also think that a knob of margarine melted into soya milk helps give a creamy flavour and texture. Don't be tempted to reduce the fats or oils in recipes – use them with a generous hand.

JAPANESE RECIPES

I have tried to keep the number of different specialist ingredients to a minimum in these recipes, but feel free to seek out sake, mirin, rice vinegar and dashi for the Japanese dishes if you like – the dishes will be all the more authentic for them. The recipes tell you where you can use these ingredients.

It really is a good idea to get the best quality soy sauce – use a naturally-brewed Japanese-style soy rather than cheaper types which may have additives and will tend to make food salty without imparting a rounded flavour. Most large supermarkets and healthfood stores offer good quality soy sauces.

When a recipe calls for ginger juice, use your garlic crusher to squeeze a few drops from a little piece of peeled ginger, without letting any of the solid matter fall through. Use the same principle for garlic juice.

SEAWEED – THE FIRST BITE

Seaweed does have a different texture and flavour from the vegetables we are accustomed to in the west, but when it comes to it, a first taste of seaweed is really no odder than anything else – do you remember the surprise of your first olive?

None of the recipes here contains challenging quantities of solid seaweed to munch through. However, if you are unsure about the taste and texture and are cooking seaweeds for the first time, try using about two-thirds of the stated quantity. That way you will just get an intriguing hint of seaweed flavour and no more.

Seaweed really is just another useful and interesting ingredient in the larder – no more and no less – to be used just as you would any other vegetable. Certainly the best way to use it at first, is as an ingredient or flavouring in a dish rather than to serve up great platefuls which look like a beach at low tide. After all, if you were presented with a dish piled high with sautéed garlic cloves for the first time, you would swiftly decide that garlic was not for you.

Seaweed comes in many different varieties, and it is interesting to exploit these different qualities and to find the uses that suit each variety best. Use hijiki for richness and texture, arame for a mild delicacy, laver to produce a gentle marine flavour and dulse for salty ocean savouryness....

SEAWEED AS A HEALTH FOOD

All kinds of claims have been made about the health benefits of eating seaweed, and although this is not the place for an investigation into the world of health supplements and wonder foods, it is quite interesting to take a glance at the nutrients in different species.

Without doubt, seaweed is an excellent food – high-fibre, low-calorie and full of vitamins, minerals and trace elements.

It is also low in fat, which is good news for western diets, unhealthily rich in heart-clogging fats. Unfortunately, it is probably because seaweed is low-fat that it marries so well with butter and oil. If you are looking at healthy eating, perhaps use cold-pressed olive oil where possible.

Some varieties of seaweed are particularly rich in vitamin C – dulse when fresh, weight-for-weight has half the vitamin C of oranges (the reason, maybe why Viking seafarers chewed it to keep scurvy at bay). And for anyone who has ever wondered how Eskimos in the bleak winter Arctic got their vitamin C, the answer is seaweed, especially laver which is a better source even than dulse. Alaria, sea lettuce, wakame, hijiki and different types of kelp are other good vitamin C providers.

Sea lettuce, alaria, kelp, wakame and hijiki are good for vitamin A and certain B vitamins. Many seaweed varieties also contain valuable quantities of minerals, such as iodine (which is probably why goitre is so rare in Japan). And some seaweed, especially laver, is a surprisingly good source of protein.

SOURCES OF SEAWEED
The one question everyone asks is – where do you get your seaweed? The answer is, for the most part at the local market, the fishmonger and the healthfood store. I also gather it from the wild.

GATHERING WILD SEAWEED
Finding and gathering seaweed is fun, and surprisingly easy.

Not all seaweeds you find on the beach are good to eat or are worth bothering with, however as with all wild food-gathering, the rule is to err on the side of caution, take your identification guide, and concentrate on seeking out a few species you know you can identify and are likely to enjoy. Most of the popular food varieties – carragheen, dulse, sugar kelp (sweet kombu), tangle (kombu) and sea lettuce are simple to recognise.

Spring and early summer are the best times to go gathering, when most seaweeds are young, luxuriant and tender. In winter, they can get rather tough, battered and strongly flavoured.

I suggest wearing wellingtons or stout boots with non-slip soles for seaweed hunts – clambering bare-foot over barnacle-encrusted rocks can be a painful experience. I also like to wear rubber gloves for plunging hands into the crepuscular corners of rockpools, though you may well dismiss this as namby-pamby advice. Do remember to take a bag or basket, which you can hook over your arm to hold the specimens, leaving two hands free for picking and balancing.

It is important that the shore and waters where you pick are unpolluted and well away from sewage outfalls. (Happily, coastal waters and beaches are becoming cleaner as local authorities respond to environmental problems; you can get information and advice on local water quality from the Environmental Health office, or from a nearby tourist information office.) In any event, avoid any unclear, smelly, muddy or oily areas of coast.

- Choose a rocky stretch of coastline; one with lots of rockpools is ideal, and arrive an hour or so before low tide so you can follow the tide out. Be sure you understand the tide patterns and are not in danger of being cut off or stranded.
- Look for plants that are still growing and attached to their rocks – leave old specimens that have been washed up on the beach (you don't know how long they have been floating about in the water), or anything discoloured, disintegrating, bleached, dried up, tatty, doubtful-smelling or in any way suspect.
- When you find your specimen, cut through the stipe, or stem, leaving plenty behind so the plant can regenerate. Never drag away the whole plant along with its holdfast, the disc – or root-like structure which secures its to the rock. Practise good conservation, by taking just a few plants from each area, leaving more than you take, and replacing any rocks you overturn.
- If you are interested in having some expert help and advice on seaweed-gathering, I know of one course organiser at the present time. Naturalist Martin Catt offers a range of themed walks, courses and short hotel-based holiday breaks on the South Devon coast, including one called Nature's Wild Harvest – Edible and Useful Plants and Seaweeds; phone (01548) 511443. I am told there may be future courses at Field Studies Council centres, too; phone (01743) 850674.

WHAT TO LOOK FOR:

Carragheen (*Chondrus crispus*). This is very common all around the coastline of Europe and North America, a pretty, frilly tuft of a plant, usually dullish red or brown, sometimes purplish, or even greenish yellow where it is exposed to strong sunlight. Up to 15cm (6") tall with delicate subdivided fronds 1-2.5 cm/1½-1" wide, the plant grows from a small flat, disc-shaped holdfast, with a very short, or non-existent central stalk. Sometimes the fronds are profusely divided into pairs of round-ended branches, although in exposed areas the fronds may be quite thin with small paired divisions.

Carragheen grows on stones in the middle to lower shore zone. I have found it especially common in rock pools, where it sometimes forms dense carpets. It often grows alongside a very similar seaweed *Gigartina stellata*, or false carragheen. The main difference between the two is that *Gigartina*'s fronds become inrolled or channelled, while carragheen's lie flat. I don't bother to distinguish between the two – both plants are good for jelly-making – *Gigartina* was used for producing a substitute for Japanese agar, for culturing bacteria in laboratories, during the second world war.

After harvesting rinse very thoroughly in several changes of water to remove grit and stray wildlife (periwinkles love to lurk in carragheen). Then lay the seaweed out in the open air to dry, and bleach to crispy creamy pink clusters.

Dulse (*Palmaria palmata*). This is my favourite edible seaweed, and it is common all around Britain and along the Atlantic coasts of North America and Europe and the northern shores of the Mediterranean. It is reddish brown to dark red, sometimes with a pretty purplish tint. Its fronds are wedge shaped, up to 30cm/12" long, flat, tough, leathery and thin, growing directly out of a

discoid holdfast. The fronds are up to 2.5cm (1") wide dividing at the ends into two or more segments. Older specimens often have leaflets growing along their margins.

Dulse grows on the lower parts of the seashore attached to rocks or other seaweeds, and it is also found below the low tide line along with the kelps.

After harvesting rinse thoroughly then boil and use fresh; or wind and air dry the plants by hanging on the washing line. Don't allow the leaves to bleach. Remember that this seaweed remains pliable even when it is thoroughly dried.

Kelps, such as tangle (*Laminaria digitata*) and sugar kelp (*Laminaria saccharina*), are brown seaweeds, commonly found around the coast of Europe and North America (especially the Atlantic seaboard). Tangle has unmistakable, great, glossy, fan-shaped fronds, up to 3m/9ft long and 90cm /3ft wide, each gingerish brown "leaf" split into a broad fringe of finger-like sections and attached to the root-like holdfast with a tough, round stem. The 3m /9ft long crinkly edged ribbon of the sugar kelp is also quite distinctive.

Both of these large seaweeds attach themselves to rocks on or below the low water-line, often forming dense carpets at the water's edge. Explore the deeper rock pools at low tide for kelps, or wade into the water; or you might find fresh specimens tossed up onto the shores still attached to their rocks.

After harvesting rinse then use fresh, or hang out to dry on the washing line or in a cool dry place. Do not worry about the sweet, white efflorescence that forms on the sugar kelp – this is mannitol, a form of sugar. Kelp is especially good for pickle making.

Laver (*Porphyra spp*).This seaweed can be found around the coast of North America, Britain and, parts of Europe. In Britain it is particularly common from autumn to spring.

Laver is green when young, becoming rosy purple then very dark brown as it ages. It can also be pale greenish brown in summer if it becomes bleached by dry weather, whereas in winter it looks like wet black silk clinging to the rocks. The fronds are up to 25 cm/10" long, a double layer of broad, delicately thin, wavy-edged "leaves" growing out from a tiny central discoid holdfast.

LAVER

Laver grows in all kinds of coastal conditions and throughout the intertidal area, but it especially likes rough, boulder-strewn beaches.

After harvesting rinse thoroughly in several changes of water, then boil to a purée which can be eaten fresh or frozen and kept for 2-3 months. Alternatively, dry and toast very lightly under a low grill or in a cool oven before storing in an airtight container.

Sea lettuce (*Ulva lactuca*). This seaweed is common all over the world and it is worth collecting just for its splashy colour – the pale, tender, green young plants mature to a brilliant vivid green, before darkening somewhat with age.

The fronds of sea lettuce are very delicate and thin, wavy edged and can be as wide as they are long. They may grow to 45cm/18" in Europe, even longer in North America, though you are more likely to find much smaller specimens. Unlike the double-layered laver fronds, sea lettuce fronds cluster in single layers around the tiny central holdfast.

Sea lettuce grows on rocks, stones and mudflats, especially on the middle and lower parts of the shore and in sheltered bays. Be warned, this seaweed has a predilection for sewage outfalls, so watch where you pick!

After harvesting rinse thoroughly, then use fresh or dry and toast very lightly under a low grill or in a cool oven before storing in an airtight container. Alternatively, cook to a purée and freeze.

Hebridean Dulse Broth
Duileasg Bree

This creamy broth comes from the Hebrides, off the coast of north-west Scotland, where seaweed has always played a part in traditional diets and is still harvested on a small scale. Serve this soup piping hot with crisp little oatcakes, and an extra knob of butter floating on the top of each bowl, or with crusty bread and cheese as a supper dish.

25 g (1 oz) dried dulse

1 medium potato (about 175 g /6 oz)

50 g (2 oz) butter

½ -1 tsp lemon juice

salt and freshly ground black pepper

750 ml(1¼ pt) milk

lemon wedges, to garnish

oatcakes, to serve

Put the dried dulse in a bowl, cover with water and leave to soak for about 5 minutes. Drain, place in a saucepan, cover with water and boil for about 10 minutes. Meanwhile peel and boil the potato, and mash thoroughly. When the dulse is cooked, drain it thoroughly. Then, beat in the mashed potato, 25 g (1 oz) of the butter and 2.5 ml (½ tsp) of lemon juice. Season with freshly ground black pepper and salt. Gradually stir in the milk. Return saucepan to heat and simmer gently for another 20 minutes, stirring often. Check seasoning and add a little extra lemon juice if you like, before pouring into individual bowls. Pop a little knob of butter on each bowl and swirl slightly, then garnish with lemon wedges. Serve with warmed oatcakes.

Serves 3-4 (or 2 as a supper dish)

Welsh Laver Soup
Cawl Lafwr

Laver seaweed is a traditional Welsh speciality. It is still sold by fishmongers in local markets, ready-cooked as a thick, black-green purée known, for some unfathomable reason, as laverbread. In this traditional recipe, laver is combined with fragrant fish stock and butter-fried vegetables to produce a hearty soup. It is worth taking the trouble to make proper flavoursome stock for this dish (you can buy quite good freshly made stock in cartons from large supermarkets if you are short of time) and don't be tempted to cut down on the generous quantities of butter. You can use ready-made fresh or canned laver purée, or make your own from dried Japanese laver (nori) – see Cook's Guide to Seaweed, page 16.

FISH STOCK

4 spring onions

1 medium carrot

50 g (2 oz) butter

1 kg (2 lb) fish trimmings, or 500 g (1lb)
    cheap white fish

1.2 litres (2 pt) water

200 ml (7 fl. oz) dry white wine

1 bouquet garni

SOUP

1 medium onion

1 medium-large potato

1 medium carrot

75 g (3 oz) butter

75 g (3 oz) cooked laver (nori)

salt and freshly ground black pepper

crusty bread, to serve

First, make the fish stock. Roughly chop the spring onions and carrot. Melt the butter in a large saucepan, add the chopped vegetables and cook until they start to soften. Add the remaining stock ingredients and simmer gently for 30 minutes, skimming the surface occasionally to remove any scum. Meanwhile, chop the onion, potato and carrot. Melt the remaining butter in a frying pan, add the onion, potato and carrot and cook for 10 minutes, stirring, until they start to colour. Remove the stock from the heat and strain it to remove fish trimmings, vegetables and bouquet garni. Return the stock to the saucepan and stir in the onion, potato and carrot, and the laver. Return the saucepan to the heat and simmer for 25 minutes. Season with salt and freshly ground black pepper, Place the soup in a food processor and process it to a medium consistency. For a fine consistency, use a blender or sieve. Recheck and adjust the seasoning, then return the soup to the saucepan and bring to simmering point. Serve with crusty bread.

Variation
Another traditional laver soup, just as good, is based on mutton stock instead of fish (use lamb stock). For a vegetarian version, use a very well-flavoured vegetable stock.

Serves 4-6

Japanese Chicken Soup

When I first made this delicate clear soup, I could not believe it would taste as good as it does with no flavourings other than Japanese kelp (kombu), chicken and vegetables cooked in plain water. The results, however, are purely delicious. Tofu (bean curd) is available from most large supermarkets and healthfood stores.

5 shiitake mushrooms, fresh or dried

1 chicken breast fillet

10 cm (4") piece of dried Japanese kelp (kombu)

1 tbs round-grain white rice

1 smallish carrot

1 small leek

125 g (4 oz) firm tofu (bean curd)

5-6 small young spinach leaves

75 g (3 oz) fine noodles

watercress sprigs or finely shredded spring onion, to garnish

If you are using dried shiitake mushrooms place these in a bowl, cover with warm water and leave to soak. Next, skin the chicken fillet and cut it into cubes. Cut the dried kombu into 6 pieces. Tie the rice firmly into a muslin cloth (a jelly bag does the job nicely). Place the chicken, kelp (kombu) and rice in a large saucepan and add 1.2 litres (2 pt) water. Bring to the boil then cover and simmer for 30 minutes, skimming the surface occasionally to remove scum. Meanwhile, cut the carrot into thin sticks, the leek into thin slices and the tofu (bean curd) into strips. Roughly tear the spinach leaves. If you are using dried shiitake mushrooms, drain them and pat dry on kitchen towel. Slice the mushrooms, removing the woody stem.

Remove the kombu from the soup and discard it. Then add the vegetables. Continue to simmer for 15 minutes. Add the fine noodles and cook for 3-4 minutes.

Serve in individual bowls: place a small pile of noodles in each bowl, then divide the tofu, chicken and vegetables among the bowls, and finally add the clear broth. Serve the rice on the side with a garnish of watercress or finely shredded spring onion.

Serves 4, or 2 as a supper dish

Cockles and Laver Gratin

Here is another traditional Welsh partnership, cockles and laver. These are sometimes served together as part of a big cooked breakfast in Wales, the laver cooked into crisp little oatmeal-coated cakes (see page 65)

You can make this recipe in one large gratin dish or four individual ramekins. For individual dishes, reduce the cooking time to 12-15 minutes.

125 g (4 oz) cooked laver purée, canned or fresh, or make your own from dried Japanese laver (nori) see (Cook's Guide to Seaweed, page 16)

2 tsp lemon juice

2 tsp olive oil

250 g (8 oz) cockles, cooked and shelled

2 tbs cream

5 g (2½ oz) fresh seasoned breadcrumbs

15 g (½ oz) butter

25-50 g (1-2 oz) well-flavoured Caerphilly or Cheddar cheese

2 tsp very finely shredded green part of a leek, to garnish, plus a few drops good quality olive oil

Preheat oven to 190°C, 375°F, Gas Mark 5. Mix together the laver, lemon juice and olive oil in a bowl, then spread the mixture over the bottom of a buttered gratin dish. In another bowl, mix together the cockles and cream and then spread them in a layer over the laver. Sprinkle the breadcrumbs over the cockles, then dot with butter and finally grate the cheese on the top. Bake at the top of the oven for about 20 minutes, until the dish is heated through thoroughly and the topping is crisp and bubbling. Toss the very finely shredded leek in a drop or two of good quality olive oil, season, then use to garnish the dish immediately before serving.

Variation

Use oatmeal for the gratin coating instead of breadcrumbs, or replace the cockles with prawns, flaked, cooked trout, salmon or any other seafood.

Serves 4

Laver and Cream Cheese Pâté

This pâté has a delicious light consistency. Add the seasonings very cautiously to avoid masking the delicate flavour of the seaweed. For a less rich paté use curd (medium-fat) cheese rather than full-fat cream cheese. You can use canned or fresh laver purée for this recipe, or make your own from dried Japanese laver (nori) -see Cook's Guide to Seaweed, page 16.

> 20 g (¾ oz) unsalted butter, softened
>
> 125 g (4 oz) cream cheese
>
> 125 g (4 oz) cooked laver purée or 15 g (½ oz)
> dried Japanese laver (nori)
>
> ½-1 tsp lemon juice
>
> freshly grated nutmeg
>
> 1 garlic clove
>
> salt and freshly ground black pepper
>
> chive leaves, to garnish
>
> oatcakes or toast fingers, to serve

Cream the butter, then beat in the cream or curd cheese until smooth. Fold in the laver. Stir in the lemon juice and a little freshly grated nutmeg, then crush the garlic clove, adding just a few drops of garlic juice to the mixture and stir. Discard the rest of the garlic clove. Season the mixture carefully with salt and freshly ground black pepper, then transfer to a serving dish. Chill for a couple of hours, garnish with chive leaves and serve with oatcakes or warm fingers of toast.

Cook's Tip

The classic way to eat laver pâté is simply to mix laver purée with a little good quality olive oil, a few drops of lemon juice, some cautious seasoning with salt and pepper and then to spread it on warm oatcakes or buttered toast fingers. Eaten like that, it tastes curiously like a mild olive paté with seafood overtones.

Serves 4

Crispy Seaweed Tempura

These crunchy little batter-coated bundles of seaweed are deep-fried then served finger-burning hot, with little bowls of richly-flavoured dipping sauce. You can use any combination of Japanese kelp (kombu), Japanese laver (nori), wakame, hijiki, dulse or arame for this adaptation of a classic Japanese recipe: I find kombu works especially well. The secret of getting the seaweed really crisp is to cut it into very thin matchsticks. Don't be tempted to prepare the batter in advance, it must be made immediately before using if it is going to be feather-light.

DIPPING SAUCE

300 ml (½ pt) well-flavoured vegetable or fish stock, or use Japanese dashi (see recipe page 13)

1 x 13 cm (5") piece Japanese kelp (kombu)

5 tsp soy sauce

1 tsp caster sugar

1 tbs sweet sherry or mirin (sweet rice wine)

TEMPURA

1 x 13 cm (5") piece Japanese kelp (kombu), dulse or wakame

1 sheet toasted Japanese laver (nori)

2 tbs hijiki or arame

1 egg

3½ tbs ice-cold water

50 g (2 oz) plain flour, plus extra for sprinkling

oil for deep frying

lemon slices and a little extra dried seaweed, to garnish

First, make the dipping sauce. Put the stock in a small saucepan. Cut the kelp (kombu) into six pieces and add it to the saucepan. Heat the stock until it boils, then simmer it for 2 minutes. Remove the kelp pieces and discard them. Then add the other sauce ingredients and simmer, stirring, until the sugar dissolves. Remove from the heat and set aside. Next, cut the kelp, dulse or wakame into very thin matchsticks – the thinner the better. Cut the nori (Japanese laver) sheet into narrow rectangles, about 4 x 1 cm (1½ x ¼"). The arame or hijiki threads are an ideal size for tempura so use them just as they are.

Next make the batter. Put the egg in a small bowl and stir in the ice-cold water. Add the flour and stir to a lumpy batter – don't try to get it smooth. Heat the oil in a deep pan or deep-fat fryer to 160°C/325°F.

Put some of the seaweed sticks into a ladle, sprinkle them with a little flour, then add 2 teaspoons of the batter and mix them together well in the ladle. Deep-fry the little seaweed bundles for 2 minutes, until golden, turning to make sure both sides cook. Meanwhile, reheat the dipping sauce. Remove the seaweed bundles from the hot oil with a slatted spoon and drain on paper towel. Serve immediately, garnished with lemon slices, with individual bowls of the warm dipping sauce.

Serves 4

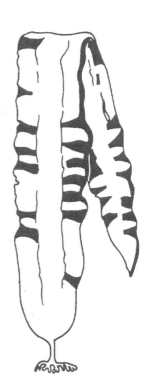

KOMBU
(Laminaria japonica)

Nori-Coated Savoury Nuts

These make a delicious snack, or nibbles with drinks. They are also good for lunch boxes, although you may want to reduce the quantity of soy sauce to make them less salty for children.

2 tsp sunflower oil

125 g (4 oz) mixed nuts (almonds, cashews, hazelnuts, peanuts...)

1 small garlic clove, finely crushed

¼ tsp paprika

1-2 tsp soy sauce

small pinch caster sugar

1 tbs green nori flakes or 1 sheet Japanese laver (nori), toasted (see Cook's Guide to Seaweed, page 15)

Heat the oil in a frying pan. Add the nuts and cook over a low heat, stirring continuously for 5 minutes. Add the garlic and paprika and cook for a further 2-3 minutes stirring continuously. Add the soy sauce and caster sugar and stir to coat the nuts thoroughly. Fry until all the liquid has evaporated. Remove the pan from the heat. If using a toasted nori sheet, cut it into very fine flakes. Add the nori to the pan and stir to coat the nuts. Transfer to a sheet of greaseproof paper and leave to cool, then store in a cool place in an airtight jar.

Makes 1 bowl

Sushi Rolls
Nori maki

These elegant little Japanese appetisers are made from rice and vegetables, rolled up in a sheet of toasted Japanese laver (nori). You can buy nori ready-toasted as sushi nori or toast it yourself (see Cook's Guide to Seaweed, page 15).

The Japanese use special bamboo sushi mats for rolling up nori maki; I find that a double layer of greaseproof paper laid on a clean folded tea towel works perfectly well.

125 g (4 oz) short-grain white rice

1½ tbs white wine vinegar or 2½ tbs rice vinegar

1 medium carrot

2 sheets toasted Japanese laver (nori)

1 tbs spinach, barely cooked

1 tbs mashed anchovy fillets

Place the rice in a saucepan with 300 ml (½ pt) salted water. Cover and bring to the boil, reduce heat and simmer for 15 minutes or until rice is soft and all the water absorbed. Set aside for 5 minutes, then transfer rice to a mixing bowl, add the vinegar and mix well. Cut the carrot into thin evenly-sized matchsticks. Lay a sheet of toasted Japanese laver (nori) on greaseproof paper. Spread half the rice over the laver, leaving a 5 cm(2") margin uncovered along the top edge. Arrange half the carrot sticks, end-to-end across the middle of the sheet, then a fine line of spinach next to them and finally a little trail of mashed anchovies. Roll up the laver tightly, like a Swiss roll, working from the bottom to the top uncovered edge. Dampen the edge, seal, then repeat the process with the second laver sheet, remaining rice, carrot, spinach and anchovies. With a sharp, wet knife cut the rolls into 2 cm (1") slices, and serve just warm or cold, but not hard and chilled, straight from the fridge.

Serves 4

Seaweed-Wrapped Tofu Bites

Tofu (bean curd) can be bought in most large supermarkets and healthfood stores. It doesn't honestly taste of much on its own, but by marinating it in garlic, onion, lemon juice and miso (savoury soya paste), then wrapping bite-size pieces in toasted seaweed sheets, it develops lots of wonderful flavour. It looks tempting too, the snowy white curd contrasting very prettily with the glossy dark-green seaweed wrapping. This is my version of a recipe by Peter and Montse Bradford; it makes perfect party food for vegetarians and vegans as well as everybody else.

1 packet firm tofu (bean curd) – about 250 g (8 oz)

2 tbs miso (savoury soya paste)

1 large garlic clove

1 tsp lemon juice

½ small onion

freshly ground black pepper

2 sheets dried Japanese laver (nori), toasted or ready-toasted

cherry tomato pieces, to garnish

Drain the block of tofu (bean curd), then wrap it up in a soft tea towel and firmly and thoroughly blot it to squeeze out all excess water (you could try putting a weight on it for 20 minutes or so). Meanwhile put 1tbs of miso in a small bowl. Crush the garlic clove and mix into the miso along with ½ tsp lemon juice. Put 1 tbs miso in another small bowl. Finely chop the onion and mix into the miso, with ½ tsp lemon juice. Season the miso marinades with freshly ground black pepper. Unwrap the tofu block and cut it in half. Coat all sides of one half-block with the garlic-miso mix, and the other half-block with the onion-miso mix. Cover and refrigerate for 24 hours. When marinated, scrape the miso mixture off the blocks (and save in a screw-top jar in the refrigerator for spreading on crackers or for stocks). Cut the blocks into 2 cm (¾") thick slices. Toast the Japanese laver (nori) sheets (see Cook's Guide to Seaweed, page 15) or use ready-toasted. Cut the nori sheets into rectangles and brush with a little water. Wrap the nori tightly around the tofu, then with a very sharp knife cut the tofu into bite-size pieces. Spear each nori-wrapped tofu cube with a cocktail stick and arrange prettily on a plate with the cherry tomato pieces.

Serves 4

Seaweed-Wrapped Crispy Chicken Bundles

This is an elegant Japanese way of serving chicken. Make sure you seal the strips of Japanese laver (nori) firmly around the chicken pieces to prevent them floating free as they cook. You can serve these little bundles simply with noodles and a vegetable dish, or as part of a larger, more elaborate Japanese meal.

250 g (8 oz) chicken breast fillet

1½ tbs soy sauce

1 tsp lemon or lime juice

1½ tbs dry sherry, or sake

1 cm (½") fresh root ginger

½ sheet dried Japanese laver (nori)

1 egg white

vegetable oil for deep frying

lime or lemon slices, to garnish

Skin the chicken and cut it into strips about 6 cm (2 ½") long and 5 mm (¼") wide. Place the strips in a shallow dish. In a small bowl mix together the soy sauce, lemon or lime juice and dry sherry or sake. Peel and finely grate the ginger, then stir into the soy sauce mixture. Pour the mixture over the chicken, stir to coat the strips thoroughly, then cover and leave to marinate for 2 hours in the refrigerator. Cut the Japanese laver (nori) into 2 cm (¾") strips. Brush each nori strip with egg white, then wrap it firmly around a bundle of 3 or 4 chicken strips. Heat the oil in a deep pan or deep-fat fryer to 180°C, 350°F. Deep-fry the chicken bundles for 2-3 minutes, or until they are crispy golden brown on the outside and cooked right through. Do not overcook them, or they will become tough. Remove them from the oil with a slotted spoon and drain on paper towel. Serve immediately, garnished with lemon or lime slices.

Serves 2-4

Roast Lamb with Rosemary and Laver Sauce

Here is another Welsh way with laver. Traditionally mutton not lamb was used, but you can't get hold of mutton these days unless you order huge amounts. Buy a half shoulder or half leg of lamb, or a larger joint if you want some left over. You can use fresh or canned laver purée, or dried Japanese laver (nori) to make your own purée (see page 16). If you can get a Seville orange for the sauce, use that and omit the lemon juice.

Lamb roasting joint
1 tsp olive oil
1 garlic clove
1 tsp lemon juice
1 tsp orange juice
fresh rosemary sprig, finely chopped
fresh thyme sprig, finely chopped
salt and freshly ground black pepper
orange slices and rosemary sprig, to garnish

LAVER SAUCE
125 g (4 oz) cooked laver
juice and finely grated peel of 1 orange
about 1 tsp lemon juice

Heat the oven to 220°C, 425°F, Gas Mark 7. Place the lamb in a roasting tray. Rub the joint with olive oil and the crushed garlic clove. Sprinkle the herbs over the joint, then the lemon juice and orange juice, and season. Cook for 45-55 minutes per kg plus 25 minutes (20-25 minutes per lb plus 25 minutes) depending on how pink you like your lamb. A few minutes before the lamb is ready, put the laver in a small saucepan and stir in the orange juice and peel. Heat gently. Take the lamb out of the oven, and stir some of the meat juices from the roasting tray into the laver sauce (saving some juices for gravy). Add extra lemon juice to taste, and adjust the seasoning. Garnish the lamb with orange slices and a sprig of rosemary, and serve with the warmed sauce.

Serves 4

Spicy Chicken and Hijiki Pancakes

The rich, substantial flavour of black hijiki seaweed marries well with the warm spices used for this savoury pancake. In fact, the stuffing mixture could equally well be used to fill pitta bread, or served just as it is with a side-dish of rice. For vegetarians, omit the chicken and double the quantity of mushrooms, stirring in the flour after you have cooked the spices for a few minutes, then gradually stirring in the sherry and apple juice.

25 g (1 oz) dried hijiki
2 tbs oil
2 medium onions
125 g (4 oz) mushrooms
175 g (6 oz) breast of chicken fillet
1 tbs plain flour
1 garlic clove, crushed
2.5 cm (1") piece of fresh root ginger
2 tsp chopped fresh coriander
½-1 tsp chilli powder
2 tsp lemon juice
1½ tbs soy sauce
3 tbs dry sherry
3 tbs apple juice
50 g (2 oz) bean sprouts
coriander leaves, to garnish

PANCAKES
175 g (6 oz) plain flour
1 large egg
200 ml (7 fl. oz) iced water
250 ml (8 fl. oz) chilled milk
oil for frying

Rinse the hijiki in running water, then place it in a bowl, cover it with water and leave it to soak for 10 minutes.

Heat the oil in a large pan. Chop up the onions and mushrooms, then sauté them in the oil for about 5 minutes. Skin the chicken fillet and cut it into small bite-size pieces.

Put the flour in a shallow bowl and roll the chicken pieces in it. Add the chicken to the pan and continue cooking for 6-8 minutes, stirring regularly. Crush the garlic clove, and peel and finely chop the ginger. Stir these into the pan along with the coriander and chilli. Continue to cook the mixture for another 5 minutes. Drain the hijiki and stir it into the mixture. Add the lemon juice, soy sauce, sherry and apple juice and continue to cook for another 8 minutes, stirring as the juices thicken. Add the bean sprouts and cook for a few minutes more. Remove the mixture from the pan and keep it warm. Put the oven to heat on a low setting.

To make the batter, sift the flour into a large bowl. Break in the egg and gradually whisk this into the flour along with the water and milk. Heat a little oil in a large frying pan, swirling the pan to make sure the oil coats the bottom. Carefully pour a ladleful of batter into the pan and tilt the pan so that the mixture spreads thinly. Cook the pancake for a few minutes until golden-brown, then turn (or flip) it over and cook the other side. Remove the pancake and keep it warm in the oven while you repeat the process. The batter should make four large pancakes, or 6-8 small ones.

Place a pancake on a warmed plate and put a tablespoonful or so of mixture in a line across it, then roll it up. Put it back in the oven. Repeat the process with the rest of the pancakes, then serve as soon as possible, garnished with fresh coriander leaves. (Pancakes can be kept warm in the oven for a while, but they are nicest eaten as soon as possible after cooking.)

Serves 2-4

Seaweed-Baked Fish Steaks

Chunky steaks of halibut or tope, layered with tomatoes, are baked on a bed of wakame seaweed. Wakame leaves are folded over the fish too, to keep in the moisture and flavour. This recipe is just as good with cod, haddock or fresh tuna, and instead of exotic Pacific wakame you can use traditional Atlantic alaria, or dabberlocks, a closely related species.

25 g (1 oz) dried wakame

4 ripe tomatoes

4 tope or halibut steaks

half an unwaxed lemon

2 tbs tomato juice

2 tsp soy sauce

2 tbs water

salt and freshly ground black pepper

1 tsp chopped fresh basil (or use ½ tsp dried)

2 tsp olive oil

fresh basil leaves, to garnish

Wash the wakame under running water, then place it in a bowl and cover it with water. Leave it to soak for about 5 minutes. Heat the oven to 200°C, 400°F, Gas Mark 6. Butter an ovenproof dish. Slice the tomatoes and arrange half of the slices in the bottom of the dish, then place all but 2 of the wakame leaves in a layer on top. Arrange the tope or halibut steaks on the bed of wakame. Finely grate the rind of the lemon and sprinkle over the fish. Squeeze the juice of the lemon over the fish, then pour over the tomato juice, soy sauce and water. Season the fish with a little salt and freshly ground black pepper, then fold the remaining two wakame leaves over the fish. Arrange the remaining tomatoes on top of the seaweed, sprinkle on the basil, then drizzle the olive oil over the top. Cover the dish with aluminium foil and bake in a preheated oven for 20-25 minutes. Garnish with fresh basil leaves and flash-grilled cherry tomatoes.

Serves 4

Kedgeree with Laver

Kedgeree was an 18th-century Anglo-Indian invention, originally a spicy mixture of rice and vegetables which, with the addition of smoked fish, later became popular as a Victorian breakfast dish. Of course, there is nothing traditional about adding seaweed to kedgeree, but laver marries well with the smoky flavour of the fish and adds a pretty green fleck to the rice. Some kedgeree recipes are highly seasoned with curry spices, but these would mask the delicate marine flavour of the laver so this version is flavoured simply with butter, aromatic basmati rice and a few cardamoms. If you want a stronger seaweed flavour, increase the quantity of laver to 175 g (6 oz).

175 g (6 oz) basmati rice

450 ml (¾ pt) water

4 cardamoms, lightly crushed

2 hard-boiled eggs

125 g (4 oz) laver purée or 15 g (½ oz) dried Japanese laver (nori) (see Cook's Guide to Seaweed, page 16)

50 g (2 oz) butter

450 g (1 lb) smoked haddock, fresh or defrosted, skinned

2 tsp lemon juice

Put the rice in a sieve and rinse it well under running water, then put it in a saucepan which has a tightly fitting lid. Add the water and the cardamoms. Bring the water to the boil, then reduce it to a low simmer and make sure the saucepan lid is firmly in place. Cook for about 6 minutes, without taking the lid off. Remove the saucepan from the heat, without removing the lid, and set it aside. Peel the eggs and chop up the egg white and yolk separately. Put the laver in a sieve to drain. Meanwhile, melt the butter in a large frying pan and gently sauté the fish for about 5 minutes until it breaks into flakes with a fork. Remove the cardamoms from the rice, then stir in the rice, egg white, laver purée (keeping back about 1 tbs for garnish) and lemon juice. Transfer the mixture to a heated serving dish and garnish it with the chopped egg yolk and the remaining laver purée arranged in stripes across the dish.

Serves 3-4

Icelandic Haddock with Dulse and Pickle Croustades

This looks quite stunning – snowy white haddock sprinkled with red-black dulse, and little croustades filled with pickle mayonnaise, rich pink from the beetroot. The recipe is an adaptation of an Icelandic supper dish which Alan Davidson includes in his excellent book North Atlantic Seafood. *Don't be put off by the fact that the haddock is served cold – it is surprisingly delicious that way, but be careful not to overcook it; it must remain very tender, moist and succulent.*

Traditionally the boiled roe of the haddock would be sliced and served along with the fish, but you may have problems getting hold of that. You can use cod's roe instead if you like – get it ready-cooked from the fishmonger.

750 g (1½ lb) haddock
5 tbs milk
15 g (½ oz) butter
salt and freshly ground black pepper
10 g (½ oz) dried dulse

CROUSTADES
125 g (4 oz) fresh fine breadcrumbs
75-125 g (3-4 oz) butter

PICKLE MAYONNAISE
4 tbs good mayonnaise
2 tbs mild made mustard (I use American)
75 g (3 oz) pickled beetroot
75 g (3 oz) pickled gherkin
a few capers (optional)

First, make the croustades. Heat the oven to about 160°C, 325°F, Gas Mark 3, then melt the butter in a small saucepan. Use a little of the butter to lightly grease some small bun tins. Put the breadcrumbs in a mixing bowl and gradually stir the butter until the mixture starts to hold together. Press the breadcrumbs firmly into the bun tins to form about 16 cup shapes, then put the croustades in the oven to crisp for about 35 minutes. When they are removed from the oven, let them cool slightly, before removing them from the tins.

Next, poach the fish. Place it in a saucepan with the milk, then dot it with butter and season it carefully (be cautious with the salt, as dulse is itself quite salty). Bring the milk to a bare simmer and poach the fish very gently for about 5 minutes, then immediately remove it from the milk and set it aside to cool completely.

To prepare the pickle mayonnaise, mix the mayonnaise and mustard together in a small bowl. Finely chop the beetroot and gherkin and stir these into the mayonnaise mixture. When the fish is cold, slice it as carefully and neatly as you can and arrange the pieces on a serving dish. Snip the dulse into fine pieces (the easiest way to do this is to roll up a piece of dulse, then snip across the roll with a pair of kitchen scissors). Sprinkle the dulse over the haddock and set it aside in a cool place for about 30 minutes.

Immediately before serving, fill the croustades with the pickle mayonnaise, sprinkle on the capers if liked and arrange on the serving platter.

Serves 3-4

Sea Bream Steamed on Seaweed

*This Japanese-style recipe uses Japanese kelp(kombu) to give an extra,
delicate, ocean flavour to the bream as it gently steams. You can use red or
black sea bream for this recipe, or even sea bass. It is important to scale
bream carefully – ask the fishmonger to do this when he cleans the fish if you
like. Make sure you ask for the head and other trimmings, to make stock for
the sauce. To extract the juice from the ginger root, crush it in a garlic press.*

2 x 13 cm (5") pieces dried Japanese kelp (kombu)

1 sea bream, about 1 kg (2 lb)

4 tbs dry sherry or sake

salt

lemon wedges and very finely chopped
   spring onion, to garnish

SAUCE

fish trimmings

600 ml (1 pt) water, plus 1 tbs for the cornflour

1 bay leaf

4 peppercorns

3 spring onions

1 x 13 cm (5") piece dried Japanese kelp (kombu)

1 tbs soy sauce

4 tbs dry sherry

2 tsp lemon juice

2 cm (¾") piece of fresh root ginger

2 tbs cornflour

To make the sauce, first make a fish stock. Place the fish trimmings in
a saucepan and add the water, bay leaf and peppercorns. Roughly chop
the spring onions and add these. Heat it until the stock boils, then
gently simmer for about 20 minutes, skimming the surface to remove
any scum. Strain the stock carefully, then return it to the rinsed
saucepan and boil it until it is reduced by about a quarter. Add the
piece of Japanese kelp (kombu) and simmer for about 5 minutes, then

remove and discard the kombu. Remove the saucepan from the heat. Stir in the soy sauce, sherry and lemon juice. Peel the ginger root and crush it, adding the juice to the sauce. Mix the cornflour with 1 tbs water to make a paste, then stir it into the sauce. Return the saucepan to the heat and cook for 1 minute, stirring, until the sauce thickens. Set the sauce aside.

Put the two remaining pieces of kombu in a bowl, cover them with water and allow them to soak just long enough for them to unfold. Rinse the bream under running water, then pat it dry with paper towels. Place a piece of kombu flat on a medium-sized plate or shallow bowl, then put the bream on top. Season the fish sparingly with salt, then lay the other piece of kombu over the bream, then pour the dry sherry over. Wrap the plate tightly in aluminium foil and place it in a steamer, or on the top of a saucepan and steam it gently for about 15 minutes. When the fish is nearly cooked, reheat the sauce. Unwrap the fish and put it on a serving dish. Pour the sauce over the fish before serving, garnished with very finely chopped spring onion and lemon wedges.

Serves 4

Savoury Rice with Arame

This aromatic vegetarian paella can be served hot or cold, as a main course (serving 3) with a crispy salad, or as a side-dish. Add saffron if you like, though you won't achieve a classic golden yellow because the arame itself colours the rice.

25 g (1 oz) dried arame
20 g (¾ oz) butter
2½ tbs olive oil
1 medium onion
250 g (8 oz) mushrooms
1 red pepper
1 small garlic clove
250 g (8 oz) rice
1 tsp paprika
½ tsp freshly grated nutmeg
600 ml (1 pt) well-flavoured vegetable stock
medium piece cinnamon stick (about 7.5 cm/3")
250 g (8 oz) peas
salt and freshly ground black pepper
50 g (2 oz) blanched almonds
fresh flat-leaf parsley leaves and 1 or 2 olives, to garnish

Rinse the arame briefly under running water, then place it in a bowl, cover it with water and leave it to soak for 5 minutes. Meanwhile, heat the butter and olive oil in a large frying pan. Finely chop the onion, mushrooms and pepper and sauté them in the oil and butter for about 5 minutes. Then crush the garlic and stir it in, along with the rice, paprika and nutmeg and cook gently for 2-3 minutes. Stir in the stock, add the cinnamon, cover and cook gently for about 6 minutes. Roughly drain the arame, then stir it into the rice, along with the peas, and continue cooking for about 4 minutes until the rice is tender and all the liquid absorbed. Remove the cinnamon stick from the rice mixture, check and adjust the seasoning. Stir in the almonds and serve garnished with fresh flat-leaf parsley and olives.

Salt Cod and Dulse

An old Icelandic way of eating dulse is to cook it with dried, salted fish, potatoes and butter. The parsnip in this dish comes from a different tradition – old English recipes often added it to stockfish (air-dried cod or other white fish) stews, to act as a sweet foil to the saltiness. You can buy salt fish from many Oriental and West Indian grocers.

1 large piece (about 600 g /1¼ lb) salted cod, ling or other white fish

1 large onion, roughly chopped

2 parsnips, roughly chopped

450 g (1 lb) potatoes, peeled and chopped

900-1200 ml (1½ -2 pt) milk

15 g (½ oz) dried dulse

25 g (1 oz) unsalted butter

freshly ground black pepper

flat-leafed parsley, to garnish

crusty brown bread, to serve

Wash the fish under running water, then place it in a bowl and cover with cold water. Leave it in a cool place overnight. Next day drain the fish, place it in a saucepan, cover it with plenty of fresh water and bring to the boil. Skim off any scum, then simmer gently for 1¼ hours. Drain, discarding the cooking water and transfer the fish to a plate to check for and discard any bones. Rinse the saucepan, then replace the fish, adding the chopped vegetables and the milk. Bring to the boil, then reduce to a simmer, cover the saucepan and cook for a further hour, or until the fish is completely tender and disintegrating and the liquid has thickened nicely. If the mixture is too thick at this point, add a little more milk. Next, add the dulse to the pan (no need to soak it) and cook for about 10 minutes, then remove from the heat, stir in the butter and season with freshly ground black pepper. Transfer to a serving dish, garnish with flat-leaf parsley and serve with crusty brown bread.

Serves 4

Wakame-Wrapped Sardines with Horseradish and Yoghurt

A seaweed wrapping seals in all the rich natural juices of these tasty little fish. Wakame seaweed is ideal – its soft and tender leaves fold tightly around the fish, while its delicate flavour gently enhances that of the sardines. Don't worry about boning the fish; once cooked, the flesh lifts cleanly away from the bones. Use alaria (dabberlocks) in place of wakame if you can get it.

6 x 13 cm (5") pieces dried wakame
12 fresh or defrosted sardines
1 tsp lemon juice
25 g (1 oz) butter
2 tbs water

FILLING
2 tbs Greek yoghurt
4 tsp horseradish sauce
4 tsp sesame seeds
2 tsp dill weed
1 tsp lemon juice
1 garlic clove

Rinse the wakame under running water, then place it in a bowl and cover it with water. Leave it to soak for 10 minutes. Heat the oven to 200°C, 400°F, Gas Mark 6. Clean and gut the sardines: with a sharp knife, remove the heads just below the gills, then make a cut along the undersides and remove the insides. Sardines are easy to scale: simply run your finger down the sides of the fish from tail to head and the scales will come away (don't use the blunt edge of a knife on these delicate little fish). Rinse thoroughly under running water, then pat dry on paper towel. Next, make the filling. Stir together the yoghurt, horseradish sauce, sesame seeds, lemon juice and dill in a small bowl. Crush the garlic clove and add just the garlic juice to the mixture. Add a little freshly ground black pepper. Drain the wakame, then place it on a board, cut away the central rib and cut each of the six leaves in half. Put a teaspoonful of the filling in the cavity of each fish, then carefully wrap a piece of wakame around each one. Make sure that the seaweed tightly seals in the filling. If the wakame leaf is deeply lobed, you may have to wind it around the fish. Tuck the seaweed-wrapped sardines snugly into an oven-proof dish. Sprinkle the lemon juice over the fish, then add a little dab of butter to each and finally sprinkle with the water. Cover the dish with foil and bake for about 20 minutes, checking half-way through and adding more water if it seems too dry.

Variation
Use the same seaweed wrapping and filling for herrings, mackerel, or fresh pilchards if you can get them.

Serves 4-6

Prawns in a Carragheen Aspic

You really ought to use fresh shellfish for this recipe, but if you have to buy frozen, get them unshelled, as they will have better flavour than ready-shelled. You could use shrimps, Dublin Bay prawns or crab in place of prawns, or colourful vegetables for a vegetarian aspic. Serve with summer herb salad (rocket, golden marjoram, sorrel, young spinach, lemon balm, chives, lamb's lettuce...); or warm potato salad with new potatoes and fresh chopped dill.

15 g (½ oz) dried carragheen

600 ml (1 pt) water

1 bay leaf

6 peppercorns

2 cloves

piece of lemon peel

2 parsley sprigs

300 g (10 oz) fresh cooked prawns

flat-leafed parsley

1 tsp red wine vinegar

2 tsp dry white wine

salt

GARNISH
dill leaves or samphire
one or two unshelled prawns
a curl of lemon peel

Put the dried carragheen in a basin, cover it with water and leave it to soak for about 5 minutes. Then, rinse it thoroughly under running water before placing it in a saucepan with the water, bay leaf, peppercorns, cloves, lemon peel and parsley sprigs. Bring to the boil, cover and simmer until it thickens. Shell the prawns, but keep back one or two unshelled for garnish. Arrange one of two leaves of parsley in the bottom of a wetted mould, then arrange half the prawns on top. Arrange a few more parsley leaves around the edge of the mould then the rest of the prawns. Stir the wine vinegar, wine and a pinch of salt into the thickened aspic, then strain the aspic through a jelly bag into the mould, making sure it runs right to the bottom of the mould. Leave to cool and set, for about 3 hours. Garnish with extra prawns and one or two leaves of flat-leafed parsley, dill or samphire and a curl of thinly sliced lemon peel.

Serves 4

Stuffed Sewin with Laver Sauce

This traditional Welsh dish combines sewin or sea trout, with a delicate laver sauce. Sewin is a delicious fish, with a flavour somewhere between salmon and trout but with the tone of a wild salmon. It is expensive and not always easy to get hold of but the recipe works very well using a small salmon, or a king rainbow trout instead. You can use fresh or canned laver purée, or make your own purée using dried Japanese laver (nori) (see Cook's Guide to Seaweed, page 16).

1 sewin (sea trout), about 1 kg (2 lb);
   cleaned, with head removed if you prefer
rosemary sprigs
3 bacon rashers
3 tbs orange juice
2 tsp lemon juice
orange slices and fresh rosemary
   sprig, to garnish

STUFFING
1 leek
1 bacon rasher
25 g (1 oz) butter
125 g (4 oz) fresh breadcrumbs
1 tbs chopped fresh parsley
1 tsp chopped fresh rosemary
2 tsp lemon juice
freshly ground black pepper

LAVER SAUCE
125 g (4 oz) laver purée
25 g (1 oz) butter
juice of 1 orange
1 tsp lemon juice

Set the oven to 200°C, 400°F, Gas Mark 6. To make the stuffing, finely chop the leek and the bacon, then melt the butter in a frying pan. Sauté the leek until it softens, then add the bacon and continue to sauté until the bacon is cooked but not brown. Stir in the breadcrumbs and herbs and continue to cook for another 3-4 minutes, stirring to prevent the breadcrumbs sticking. Stir in the lemon juice and season with a little black pepper.

Place the trout in a baking dish and fill the cavity with the stuffing mixture. Sprinkle little sprigs of rosemary over the fish. Stretch the bacon rashers with the back of a knife, then wrap them around the trout to pull together the cavity and keep the stuffing in place. Sprinkle over the fruit juices, then seal the baking dish carefully with foil and cook the trout for about 25 minutes, until just tender. Check occasionally to make sure that the fish has not dried out, and be very careful not to overcook it. If the fish is virtually cooked but the bacon has not crisped up, open up the foil, baste the fish and place the dish under a medium grill for a minute or two.

To make the laver sauce, put the laver purée in a fine sieve and leave it to drain for a few minutes. Melt the butter in a small saucepan, and stir in the laver and fruit juices. Serve the fish, garnished with orange slices and a fresh rosemary sprig, and with a side dish of the warm sauce.

Serves 4

Spaghetti with Dulse Pesto

This makes a quick, tasty vegetarian dish, with the dulse adding an intriguing, subtle ocean flavour to the sauce. If you like, you can make your pesto sauce from scratch, by pounding a bunch of basil with pine kernels, garlic, Parmesan and olive oil, which is delicious but more laborious than this easy method. Serve with a crisp mixed-leaf salad.

40 g (1½ oz) dried dulse

2 tbs olive oil, plus 1 tsp for the spaghetti

50 g (2 oz) pine kernels

2 garlic cloves

half a dozen fresh basil leaves

200 g (7 oz) green pesto sauce

freshly ground black pepper

**600-750 g (1-1½ lb) spaghetti, depending
on appetites**

freshly grated Parmesan cheese, to serve

Place the dulse in a bowl, cover it with water and leave it to soak. Heat
the olive oil in a frying pan. Add the pine kernels and fry them until
they start to colour. Crush the garlic cloves and add these to the pan.
Continue to cook for about 4 minutes, taking care not to brown the
garlic. Roughly tear the basil leaves (set aside a couple for garnish) and
add them to the pan, then stir in the pesto sauce and cook for a
minute more. Remove the dulse from the bowl of water (do not drain
too thoroughly, as a little extra liquid is needed in the sauce) and stir it
into the pesto mixture. Continue to cook for a minute more, stirring
until the dulse is finely broken up, then season with black pepper.
Remove the sauce from the heat and keep it warm. Cook the spaghetti
according to the instructions, in plenty of boiling water, with 1 tsp of
olive oil added to the water. When cooked *al dente*, drain the spaghetti
thoroughly and return it to the saucepan. Pour the sauce over the
spaghetti and toss well to coat it thoroughly. Divide the pasta among
four individual plates, garnish with the remaining basil leaves or parsley
and serve with a bowl of freshly grated Parmesan cheese.

Variation
For Seafood and Dulse Pesto, stir 125-175 g (4-6 oz) shelled cooked
prawns or mussels into the sauce and heat gently through before
serving.

Serves 4

Lasagne with Dulse

The dulse gives a wonderful subtle flavour to the béchamel sauce in this recipe. You could equally well use laver (nori) if you prefer. Don't worry if the sauces seem rather thin when you first make them – the extra liquid will be taken up by the lasagne as it cooks. Serve with a crisp salad. (For a speedy, but not quite so good, version of this dish, use a ready-made tomato sauce thinned with a little red wine, and a simple white sauce thinned with a little cream.)

275 g (9 oz) quick-cook lasagne
125 g (4 oz) well-flavoured Cheddar cheese

BÉCHAMEL SAUCE
25 g (1 oz) dried dulse
1 litre (1¾ pt) milk
½ onion
1 bay leaf
8 peppercorns
1 carrot
a few parsley stalks
75 g (3 oz) butter
75 g (3 oz) flour
salt and white pepper

TOMATO SAUCE
4 rashers bacon
2 tbs olive oil
2 celery stalks
1 onion
1 small carrot
125 g (4 oz) mushrooms
1 garlic clove
1 tbs chopped fresh parsley
2 tsp oregano
4 tbs red wine
1 x 400 g (14 oz) can plum tomatoes
2 tbs concentrated tomato purée
4 tbsp water
a few snips dried dulse, to garnish

Rinse the dulse under running water, then put it in a bowl and cover it with water. Leave it to soak for about 10 minutes. Make the béchamel sauce: put the milk in a saucepan, slice the onion and add it to the milk along with the bay leaf, peppercorns, carrot and parsley. Bring to boil and simmer for a moment, then remove it from the heat. Put it aside to allow the flavours to infuse. Melt the butter in a pan and stir in the flour. Cook for about 2 minutes, stirring. Strain the milk and then gradually stir it into the pan. Bring it to the boil again and cook for about 2 minutes, stirring, then set it aside.

Drain the dulse, then put it in a saucepan, cover it with water and bring to boil. Simmer for about 10 minutes, until it breaks up easily. Then drain thoroughly and chop and mash until it makes a purée. Stir the dulse into the béchamel sauce, then season with salt and white pepper.

Heat the oven to 190°C, 375°F, Gas Mark 5. Next make the tomato sauce. Put the bacon in a large frying pan and cook until the rashers begin to crisp. Then add the oil. Finely chop the celery, onion and carrot and when the oil is hot, add them to the pan and sauté. Chop up the mushrooms and add these, along with the crushed garlic clove. Cook for another 5 minutes, then stir in the parsley, oregano, red wine and canned tomatoes. Cook for a couple more minutes, then remove the pan from the heat and chop up the bacon and tomatoes. Return the pan to the heat, stir in the tomato purée and water, season and cook for 2 minutes more.

Pour a layer of tomato sauce into the bottom of a large, preferably rectangular, oven-proof dish. Next add a layer of the lasagne, to cover the tomato sauce completely. Then carefully add a layer of béchamel sauce, then a layer of lasagne. Repeat the process, ending with béchamel sauce. Sprinkle Cheddar cheese over the top of the sauce, cover and cook in the middle of a preheated oven for about 30-35 minutes. Garnish with some finely snipped dried dulse.

Variation
For Vegetarian Dulse Lasagne, omit the bacon, add an extra 1 tbs oil for frying, and double the quantities of onion and mushrooms in the tomato sauce. Use vegetarian Cheddar for the topping.

Serves 4

Salmon and Laver Fishcakes

These tasty little fishcakes are lightly flavoured with dill and tarragon, rolled in oatmeal and then fried in butter. It is important not to overdo the herbs, or you will mask the subtle taste of the laver. You can use canned or fresh laver purée, or make your own purée from dried Japanese laver (nori); see Cook's Guide to Seaweed, page 16. Serve the fish cakes with Kelp Tartare.

125 g (4 oz) laver purée

1 medium onion

20 g (¾ oz) butter, plus extra for frying

200 g (7 oz) cooked potato

400 g (14 oz) fresh salmon lightly poached or steamed, or canned salmon

2 tsp lemon juice

½ tsp dill

½ tsp tarragon

salt and freshly ground black pepper

75-125 g (3-4 oz) oatmeal

Kelp Tartare, to serve (see page 74)

dill sprigs, to garnish; or use samphire

Place the laver purée in a fine sieve and leave it to drain. Finely chop the onion. Melt the butter in a pan, then sauté the onion until it is very soft but not coloured. Transfer the onion to a mixing bowl. Mash the potato and the drained laver purée thoroughly into the onion. If you are using fresh salmon, carefully bone and skin it, then flake it. If you are using canned fish, drain it, then add fresh or canned salmon to the mixing bowl along with the lemon juice and herbs. Gently mix the ingredients together, leaving the fish in smallish flakes. Test and adjust the seasoning (remember, laver can be quite salty, so apply any extra salt with caution). Divide the mixture into 16 and roll each into a cake shape, then roll it in oatmeal. Melt butter in a frying pan and fry the fishcakes until crisp and brown. Serve with a dish of Kelp Tartare and a garnish of dill.

Variation

Use smoked haddock or smoked cod instead of salmon to make the fishcakes. Try serving them with a light tomato sauce.

Serve 4

Savoury Stuffed Seaweed Parcels

Seaweed makes a good wrapping material for all kinds of stuffings – use Japanese laver (nori) or wakame for these savoury parcels which are delicious served with pasta and tomato sauce. (You can use vegetarian Cheddar or Pecorino in place of Parmesan if you prefer.)

6 sheets dried Japanese laver (nori) or 25 g (1 oz) dried wakame

75 g (3 oz) long grain rice

200 ml (7 fl. oz) water, plus 15 ml (1 tbsp) for sprinkling

1½ tbs olive oil, plus 1 tbs for drizzling

1 onion

1 garlic clove

1½ tbs pine kernels

½ tsp oregano

½ tsp dill

1 tbs lemon juice

1 tsp soy sauce

1 tbs freshly grated Parmesan, plus a little extra for sprinkling

salt and freshly ground black pepper.

If you are using wakame seaweed, place it in a bowl, cover it with water and leave it to soak. Heat the oven to 190°C, 375°F, Gas Mark 5. Rinse the rice, then put it into a lidded saucepan with the water and bring to the boil. Reduce to a simmer and cook for about 12 minutes, depending on the variety of rice you are using, until the water is absorbed (basmati rice takes about 8 minutes; wholegrain rice 20 minutes). Heat 1½ tbs olive oil in a frying pan. Finely chop the onion, then sauté it until it softens. Crush the garlic clove, add it to the pan and continue cooking for about 5 minutes, then add the cooked rice, pine kernels and herbs and cook for a minute or two more. Remove from the heat, stir in the lemon juice, soy sauce and cheese, then test and adjust the seasoning. If you are using nori sheets, cut the 6 sheets in half. Brush a little water lightly over the pieces. Arrange about a tablespoonful of stuffing on each strip, about two-thirds of the way down it. Roll up the strip, tucking in the ends as you go. When you have rolled up the bundle, press the ends firmly, adding a little extra water if necessary to seal the parcel effectively. If you are using wakame, drain it thoroughly, keeping back 1 tbs of the soaking water. For each parcel, you need 3 strips of wakame. Lay one strip on a flat surface. Lay the second and third pieces across the first to make a star shape. Place about a tablespoonful of the stuffing in the centre of the star shape and pull the ends up over the mixture to seal it into a bundle. Arrange your 12 nori parcels or wakame bundles in an oven-proof dish. Drizzle 1 tbs olive oil over them, plus 1 tbs water. Cover and cook in a preheated oven for 20-25 minutes, checking occasionally that they do not dry out. Sprinkle with extra cheese before serving.

Variation
For a non-vegetarian alternative, fry 50-125 g (2-4 oz) minced lamb with the onion, before stirring the other ingredients into the stuffing.

Serves 4

WAKAME

Hijiki Salad

*Black strands of richly flavoured hijiki seaweed are threaded through green
and yellow vegetables in this salad. In Japan, hijiki is known as "bearer of
wealth and beauty" – here its robust taste is mellowed and sweetened by
cooking it in apple juice. This will serve 4.*

15 g (½ oz) dried hijiki
350 ml (12 fl. oz) apple juice
1 tbs soy sauce
1 small orange or yellow pepper
75 g (3 oz) cooked French beans
75 g (3 oz) cooked sweetcorn kernels
50 g (2 oz) bean sprouts
1 medium carrot
mint sprig, to garnish

DRESSING
1 tsp white distilled vinegar
1 tsp water
½ tsp dry mustard
1 tsp sugar
1 tsp soy sauce

Place the hijiki in a bowl and cover with warm water. Leave it to soak
for 10 minutes, then drain and place in a saucepan. Add the apple juice
and the soy sauce and simmer for 30-35 minutes, until the seaweed is
tender and virtually all the liquid has gone. If the liquid evaporates
before this, add a little extra apple juice or water to the pan. Remove
the hijiki from the pan and place it in a bowl, setting aside the saucepan
with the remaining cooking liquid. Cut the yellow pepper into small,
neat squares and chop the beans into smallish pieces. Add these, and
the sweetcorn and bean sprouts to the hijiki. Finely chop the carrot and
add it, mixing well to combine the ingredients. Stir all the dressing
ingredients into the remaining cooking liquid in the saucepan and heat
gently, stirring, until the sugar has dissolved. Leave the dressing to cool,
then pour over the salad and serve garnished with a mint sprig.

Mediterranean Salad with Arame Dressing

Arame is a mild-tasting Japanese seaweed which combines surprisingly well with the Mediterranean flavours of tomatoes, peppers, herbs and olive oil. Make sure that the olives are well rinsed before adding them, or their saltiness will overwhelm the other elements. And do make the dressing well in advance to allow the flavours to develop. Serves 4.

DRESSING

1 tbs extra virgin olive oil

1 tsp red wine vinegar

pinch sugar

1 garlic clove, finely crushed

½ tsp chopped fresh oregano (or large pinch of dried)

½ tsp fresh basil (or large pinch of dried)

1½ tsp pesto sauce

2 tbsp crumbled arame

salt and freshly ground black pepper

1 red pepper

1 green pepper

4 ripe tomatoes

½ frisée lettuce

50 g (2 oz) stoned black olives

large sprig marjoram

First make the dressing. In a small bowl combine the olive oil, vinegar, sugar, garlic, herbs and pesto sauce. Add the roughly crushed arame, and a little salt and freshly ground black pepper. Mix well, then cover and leave for at least 2 hours for the flavours to develop. To prepare the salad, deseed the peppers and cut them into strips; slice the tomatoes and tear up the frisée lettuce. Rinse the olives under running water in a sieve, then pat them dry on paper towels. Tear up the marjoram leaves. Combine all the ingredients in a bowl. Pour the dressing over and toss well.

Japanese Cucumber Salad

This is a classic Japanese salad which I have found goes very well with crispy fried foods. It is best served slightly chilled, so refrigerate it for 20-30 minutes before serving.

> 1 large cucumber
>
> 200 ml (7 fl. oz) water
>
> 1 tsp salt
>
> 15 g (½ oz) scant measures, dried wakame
>
> 4 cm (1½") fresh root ginger
>
> **DRESSING**
>
> 1½ tbs wine vinegar and 1½ tbs water
>
>   or 3 tbs rice vinegar
>
> 1½ tbs soy sauce
>
> 1 tbs sugar

Cut the ends off the cucumber, then peel it, leaving thin strips of peel along the length. Slice the cucumber in half lengthways and scoop out the seeds. Cut each half into fairly thin slices. Pour the water into a shallow bowl, dissolve the salt into it, then add the cucumber slices and leave them to soak for about 20 minutes. Place the wakame in a bowl, cover with warm water and leave to soak for 15 minutes.

Make the dressing. Place the ingredients in a small saucepan and warm gently, stirring, until the sugar has dissolved. Peel and coarsely grate the ginger. Place in a shallow bowl. Drain the cucumber and squeeze the slices to remove any excess moisture, then add to the ginger. Drain the wakame into a sieve, rinse with boiling water, drain and squeeze out excess water. Put the seaweed on a plate, cut off and discard any hard stems, then shred it coarsely and add to the ginger and cucumber. Mix all the salad ingredients together, then pour the dressing over and refrigerate for 30 minutes before serving.

Serves 4

Dulse Slaw

Dulse is a delicate, rosy pink seaweed which gives this salad a subtle marine flavour.

25 g (1 oz) dried dulse
50 g (2 oz) raisins
175 g (6 oz) white cabbage
1 medium carrot
2 small shallots

DRESSING
4 tbs good quality mayonnaise
2 tbs fresh apple juice
freshly ground black pepper and salt

Put the dulse in a small bowl and cover it with water. Leave it to soak for 5 minutes. Put the raisins in a small bowl, cover them with warm water and leave them to plump up for about 5 minutes. Finely chop the white cabbage, coarsely grate the carrot and very finely chop the shallots, then place the prepared vegetables in a large bowl. Drain the dulse thoroughly, chop it roughly and add it to the bowl, then drain the raisins and add these. In a small bowl mix together the dressing ingredients. Pour the dressing over the salad, then toss to mix and coat thoroughly. Season with freshly ground black pepper, then check the seasoning and add salt if necessary. Toss again and serve.

Serves 4

Arame California Salad

In this brilliantly-coloured tangy salad, shiny black strands of arame are tossed together with citrus fruits and walnuts. Avocado adds a warm creaminess to the dish while raisins give little points of sweetness. Don't drown the salad in dressing, add only enough to coat the ingredients. The flavours are greatly improved by letting this salad stand for about half an hour in a cool place before serving.

15-20 g (½-¾ oz) dried arame

25 g (1 oz) raisins

1 carrot

1-2 celery stalks

1 avocado

2 oranges

25 g (1 oz) walnut halves

DRESSING

50 ml (2 fl oz) orange juice

50 ml (2 fl oz) olive oil

1 tsp lemon juice

1 garlic clove

splash soy sauce

salt and freshly ground black pepper

Rinse the arame under running water, then place it in a bowl and cover with water. Leave it to soak for about 5 minutes. Place the raisins in a small bowl, cover them with warm water and leave them for about 5 minutes to plump up. Next, make the dressing. In a small bowl combine the orange juice, olive oil and lemon juice. Crush the garlic clove and add the juice only to the dressing. Add a splash of soy sauce and then season the dressing with a little salt and pepper. Mix the ingredients well. Then make the salad. Cut the carrot and celery into thin sticks and put them in a large bowl. Peel and cut up the avocado and oranges, removing any pips, then add to the carrot and celery. Drain the arame and raisins thoroughly and add these to the other ingredients. Finally, sprinkle with the walnuts, then pour over the dressing and toss the salad to coat thoroughly. Leave it in a cool place for about half an hour, then toss again immediately before serving.

Serves 4

Samphire with Nut-Brown Butter Sauce

The Pig'n'Fish is a restaurant in St Ives which earns an entry in the Good Food Guide, *and what better place for a restaurant specialising in fish than Cornwall? Paul Sellars, the restaurateur, suggests serving samphire with a simple butter noisette, a butter sauce made here with sherry vinegar and cooked to the colour of hazelnuts; along with perhaps a simply roasted piece of wild salmon and some baby new potatoes.*

You can cook the well-rinsed samphire in rapidly boiling water for 2-4 minutes, or steam it for 6-8 minutes. The cooking time varies according to how young and tender the plants are – test often during cooking to make sure you don't overcook it. Don't add salt to the cooking water.

1 shallot

125 g (4 oz) unsalted butter

4 tsp sherry vinegar

salt and freshly ground black pepper

2 good handfuls samphire

Rinse the samphire thoroughly under running water, then pick over it removing any old pieces and tough stalks. Next make the sauce. Chop the shallot very finely. Heat the butter carefully in a pan, skimming off any scum as it forms on the surface. Cook until the butter turns to a golden hazelnut colour (be careful not to overcook it) then add the shallot. Measure the sherry vinegar into a jug, then carefully pour the nut-browned butter from the pan into the jug, leaving behind any sediment, and whisk. Season carefully, then set the sauce aside and keep warm. Cook the samphire in plenty of boiling water, checking regularly to make sure it does not overcook.

Serves 4 as a side dish

Laverbread

This is the classic Welsh way to cook laver seaweed, as little oatmeal-coated cakes fried in the pan with crispy bacon. The secret of getting the cakes to hold together properly is to mix a little oatmeal into the laver purée, then to let it stand for 20 minutes to absorb any excess moisture. These laver cakes make an excellent brunch with grilled cherry tomatoes and butter-brushed grilled mushrooms. You can use fresh or canned laver, or dried Japanese laver (nori) boiled to a purée (see Cook's Guide to Seaweed, page 16). Try to get good-quality bacon, not the soggy pre-packaged variety. For vegetarians, simply omit the bacon and cream if you like, and fry the cakes in butter or good quality oil.

125 g (4 oz) cooked laver or 15 g (½ oz) dried Japanese laver (nori) boiled to a purée

1 tsp double cream

pinch salt

25-50 g (1-2 oz) oatmeal, plus extra for coating

4 rashers good quality streaky bacon

15 g (½ oz) butter (optional)

Put the laver in a fine sieve and allow it to drain for about 5 minutes. Then, place it in a bowl and mix it with cream, salt and about 40 g (1½oz) oatmeal to form a stiff purée. Leave it to stand for about 20 minutes, then form the laver into 8 little cakes and roll them in oatmeal. Place the bacon in a large frying pan and fry on both sides for a few minutes until the fat begins to run. Melt the butter (if you have a lot of fat from the bacon, you may decide to omit the butter). When the butter begins to sizzle, push the bacon to the edges of the pan and add the laver cakes. Fry them, turning once, until they are golden brown, and the bacon is cooked but not crisp. Remove the cakes and the bacon from the pan. Cut the rind from the rashers, then slice each rasher in half lengthways. Wrap a strip of bacon around each little laver cake. Place the cakes in a grill pan, and grill briefly until the bacon crisps up nicely, then serve.

Serves 4

Tsawatainuk Corn and Laver

Judith Cooper Madlener includes a recipe for "gluckastan", a Native American dish, in The Sea Vegetable Book *and I came upon it in the Maine Coast Sea Vegetables recipe booklet. Apparently, the people of the Tsawatainuk tribe in British Columbia harvested the local laver and cooked it up with maize. Below is my version of the recipe (you can use ready-made creamed corn if you like, but I prefer to cream the corn myself with milk and butter).*

I served my corn and laver as a side dish to enchiladas, (rolled flour tortillas, stuffed with a vegetarian chilli sauce and covered with melted cheese and soured cream) along with home-made refried beans and an avocado salad. This combination isn't at all traditional – tortillas come from California-Mexican border country, whereas the Tsawatainuk Indians and gluckastan are from the Pacific Northwest, but that doesn't make it any the less delicious.

15 g (½ oz) dried laver (nori) and 200 ml (7 fl. oz) milk or 125 g (4 oz) cooked laver purée and 4 tbsp milk

400 g (14 oz) canned or defrosted sweetcorn kernels

15 g (½ oz) butter

freshly ground black pepper

If you are using dried laver (nori), first toast the sheets over a flame (see page 15), then crumble them into a bowl. Cover with the milk, keeping back 2 tbs for the corn, and leave the seaweed to soak for about 5 minutes. If you are using ready-made laver purée, place the laver in a fine sieve for about 5 minutes to drain off any excess liquid. Place the corn kernels and 2 tbs milk in a food processor and whiz for a few seconds. Not all the kernels should be cut up – some should remain whole. Place the processed corn in a saucepan, along with the soaked laver or laver purée and any remaining milk, and simmer gently for about 5 minutes, or until the laver has disintegrated. Add extra milk if the mixture seems too dry. Stir in the butter and season with freshly ground black pepper before serving.

Variation
For a spicy version of this dish, fry a finely chopped small red chilli

pepper for about 4 minutes in a little butter or oil, then stir it into the corn and laver mixture before simmering.

Serves 4

Crispy Fried Seaweed

This traditional Chinese dish has the distinction of being the only seaweed recipe in this book to have no seaweed in it! Cabbage, which is always used in place of seaweed for this classic dish, is shredded up and cooked to look like Chinese "hair" seaweed. It really works – as you toss the handfuls of cabbage into the hot oil, the strands quickly begin to curl and turn to a crispy dark translucent green, just like seaweed. By all accounts, cabbage has a lot more flavour than real "hair seaweed", but no doubt you could use proper seaweed if you really wanted to.

450 g (1 lb) spring greens

50 g (2 oz) flaked almonds

600 ml (1 pt) mild-flavoured cooking oil

1 tsp caster sugar

large pinch salt

Wash the spring greens, then drain them and shred them very finely. Spread them out on tea towels to dry, turning them occasionally. Place the almonds in a grill pan and toast them lightly for a few minutes under a medium grill. When the greens are absolutely dry, heat the oil in a large frying pan. Remove it momentarily from the heat and throw in the greens. Return the pan to the heat and stir-fry the greens for about 3 minutes. Remove them with a slotted spoon and drain them on paper towels. Place the crispy seaweed in a serving dish, then sprinkle with the sugar and salt. Sprinkle with the toasted almonds and serve immediately.

Serves 4 as a side dish

Stir-Fried Vegetables with Arame

The delicate black threads of arame add contrast and an interesting subtle flavour to the stir-fried vegetables. Arame is a mild tasting seaweed, but if you are unsure about it, use 15 g (½ oz) the first time you make this.

20 g (¾ oz) dried arame
175 g (6 oz) broccoli
1 medium onion
1 large carrot
175 g (6 oz) mushrooms
4 Chinese leaves
2 tbs oil
1 garlic clove
5 tsp apple juice
1 tbs soy sauce
½ tsp sugar
large pinch salt
1 tsp sesame seeds

Wash the arame under running water, then place it in a bowl and cover it with water. Leave it to soak for 5 minutes. Break the broccoli into smallish florets and put them in a pan of boiling water. Cook them for 2 - 3 minutes, then drain them under cold running water to refresh them. Cut up the onion and cut the carrot into thin sticks. Slice up the mushrooms and finely chop the Chinese leaves. Heat the oil in a frying pan and stir in the onion and carrot. Stir-fry for about 2 minutes, add the broccoli and stir-fry for 2 minutes. Crush the garlic clove and add it, along with the mushrooms and the arame. Add the apple juice, soy sauce, sugar and salt and continue to cook for about 4 minutes. Stir in the Chinese leaves and cook for 1 minute. Transfer the vegetables to a serving dish and sprinkle with the sesame seeds. Serve immediately.

Serves 2-4

Japanese Noodles with Seaweed

These noodles, sprinkled with green nori flakes and served with a rich dipping sauce, make an ideal accompaniment to a Japanese meal. They also go well with fish.

DIPPING SAUCE

475 ml (16 fl. oz) good vegetable, fish or chicken stock

3 tbs soy sauce

1 tbs sweet sherry or mirin (sweet rice wine)

1 tbs sugar

1 tbs hot horseradish sauce

green nori flakes, or 1 sheet dried Japanese laver (nori)

325 g (11 oz) noodles

finely chopped spring onion, to serve

First make the dipping sauce. Put the stock in a saucepan and simmer it until it is reduced by about one-third. Stir in the soy sauce, sherry, sugar and horseradish sauce and continue to simmer and stir until the sugar is dissolved. Leave to cool. Next, toast the Japanese laver (nori) sheet, if you are using it (see page 15). Then crumble it up as finely as possible. Finally plunge the noodles in a saucepan of boiling water and cook. Drain them thoroughly and put them in a bowl. Sprinkle with the green nori flakes, or toasted nori and mix thoroughly. Serve the noodles, with spring onion and with little dishes of the dipping sauce.

Serves 4

Fresh Noodles Made with Seaweed

Seaweed has a wonderful affinity with fish, and these speckled-coloured fresh noodles are particularly delicious served with a creamy seafood sauce. Home-made noodles are quite time-consuming to prepare, but worth it for a special meal (you can make them a day in advance and keep them between leaves of greaseproof paper in the fridge). Use dulse or laver (nori). For a less-rich sauce, replace some of the cream with low-fat fromage frais, stirred in at the last minute.

25 g (1 oz) dried dulse or 125 g (4 oz) fresh or canned laver purée or 15 g (½ oz) dried Japanese laver (nori)

250-275 g (8-9 oz) strong white flour

2 medium eggs

1 tbs olive oil

pinch salt

SAUCE

900 ml (1½ pt) good fish stock

120 ml (4 fl. oz) double cream

1 tbs chopped fresh parsley

2 tsp lemon juice

175 g (6 oz) cooked salmon

175 g (6 oz) cooked haddock, cod or other white fish

50 g (2 oz) shelled cooked prawns

freshly ground black pepper and salt if wished

4 cooked prawns and dill or parsley sprigs, to garnish

First make your seaweed purée. If you are using dulse, place the dulse in a bowl, cover with water and leave it to soak for about 10 minutes. Then put it in a saucepan, cover it with fresh water and boil it for 10-

12 minutes until it is well cooked. Drain it very thoroughly, squeezing out any liquid, then rub it through a fine sieve to make a purée. If you are using laver, place the fresh or canned laver in a sieve and drain as much liquid as possible to make a dry purée, or boil the crumbled dried Japanese laver (nori) in a saucepan of water for 5 minutes, then drain very thoroughly, squeezing out as much liquid as possible. You should end up with about 50 g (2 oz) stiff seaweed purée.

Sift 250 g (8 oz) flour into a large bowl and make a well in the centre. Break in the eggs, add the oil, seaweed purée and salt and mix it thoroughly to a smooth dough. Add extra flour if it seems too sticky. Knead the dough for about 8 minutes. Sprinkle with a little extra flour and leave the dough to rest for about 1 hour, covered with a clean tea towel. Divide the dough into 4 pieces. Take one piece and on a floured board roll it out very thinly. Carefully roll up the sheet of dough into a loose roll, then slice the roll into 5 mm (¼") strips. Unravel the strips very carefully and lay them on sheets of greaseproof paper. Repeat the process with the other 3 pieces of pasta dough. Leave the noodles to dry for at least 1 hour before cooking in plenty of boiling water for 4-5 minutes, then drain immediately and keep warm.

To make the sauce, pour the stock into a saucepan and bring to the boil. Reduce the heat and simmer to reduce the liquid by about one quarter. Stir in the cream and continue simmering, stirring, until the sauce thickens. Stir in the parsley and lemon juice and cook for 1 minute. Then stir in the flaked salmon, white fish and prawns and cook gently for a minute or two more until thoroughly heated through. Before serving, check and adjust the seasoning. Arrange the noodles on individual plates, carefully pour the sauce over and garnish with prawns and dill or parsley sprigs.

Serves 2-4

Dulse Relish

Eighteenth-century Scottish and Irish immigrants to North America brought their culinary traditions with them, including various ways of using dulse and carragheen seaweed which grew just as abundantly in the western waters of the Atlantic as they had done back home.

Dulse was popular for chewing and for cooking, and dulse relish was a traditional New England appetiser. I have not been able to track down an original recipe for this – no doubt sometimes the dried dulse was simply snipped and sprinkled over a savoury dish.

Why, I asked my English dulse suppliers, did some books on seaweed stress how much boiling was needed to make dulse edible, when the kind I use is delicate and tender, requiring only a few minutes soaking and cooking? Was it pre-boiled before drying? No, the suppliers replied, their dulse is harvested from the Bay of Fundy off the east coast of North America and imported, and is naturally tender.

This relish is good served along with fish stews and other robust fish dishes, also with stir-fries. I think it works very well with sweet gammon, and cold meats, too.

15 g (½ oz) dried dulse

4 tsp sesame oil

1 onion

½ tsp salt

1 tsp sugar

1 tsp lemon juice

Put the dulse in a bowl and add just enough water to barely cover it. Leave it to soak for about 5 minutes. Heat the sesame oil in a pan. Finely chop the onion and sauté it in the oil until it is very soft, but not brown. Pour the dulse, along with its soaking water into the pan, stir in the salt, sugar and lemon juice, then cook, stirring until the dulse is finely broken up and the mixture makes a thick consistency. Transfer to a bowl and leave to cool.

Pickled Kelp

You will find dried kelp sold under its Japanese name – kombu. If you want to try local kelp, look for Atlantic or local kombu. To be honest, there is not a lot of difference between the two varieties, although it seems to me that Japanese kombu is slightly softer in texture, with a milder flavour.

Until recently you could buy pickled kelp by mail order from an Orkney firm called Ootashell, but I am told they are no longer in business. It is easy to make your own, however, and it will keep for a few weeks in a sealed jar in the fridge.

Pickled kelp tastes a bit like capers, and makes an excellent addition to seafood pizzas and tomato pasta sauces. I use it for making a tartare sauce (see page 74). You can also eat it like sauerkraut.

3 x 13 cm (5") pieces dried kelp (kombu)

200 ml (7 fl. oz) red wine vinegar

120 ml (4 fl. oz) water

3 garlic cloves

3 bay leaves

10 peppercorns

½ tsp oregano

2 tsp salt

large pinch allspice

125 g (4 oz) sugar

Put the kelp (kombu) in a bowl and cover it with water. Leave it to soak for 5 minutes. Put the wine vinegar and water in a saucepan. Peel and finely slice the garlic cloves and add to the saucepan along with the bay leaves, peppercorns, oregano, salt and allspice. Bring to a simmer, then gradually stir in the sugar. Continue to stir until all the sugar is dissolved. Cook for about 3 minutes more, then remove the saucepan from the heat. Drain the kelp and cut it up into shreds. Add these to the saucepan. Return the saucepan to the heat and simmer for about 4 minutes (the kelp must not become gelatinous). Remove the saucepan from the heat, and allow the pickle to cool slightly, then transfer it to a jar. Seal, and cool thoroughly.

Kelp Tartare

This sauce, made from pickled kelp (see page 73) makes an excellent accompaniment to fried fish dishes - even fish and chips. It's also good with burgers.

2 tbs pickled kelp

2 tbs good mayonnaise

1 tsp lemon juice

1-2 tsp milk or single cream

1 tsp snipped chives

Drain the pickled kelp and chop it up finely, then put it in a bowl. Add the mayonnaise and lemon juice and mix the ingredients together. Add milk or cream to thin it a little, then stir in the snipped chives.

Variation
Use half mayonnaise and half plain yoghurt for a lighter sauce.

Makes 1 bowl

SUGAR KELP
(Laminaria saccharina)

Dulse Black Butter

This is one of my favourite things to do with dulse – its salty ocean flavour is so good as a savoury butter. Shiny and almost black in colour, the butter looks wonderful melting richly over a pure white fillet of cod or lemon sole and a little goes a long way. (Classic black butter, *beurre noir*, is of course something completely different, a brown-coloured butter sauce traditionally served with skate.) Serve dulse black butter slightly warm.

25 g (1 oz) dried dulse

50 g (2 oz) unsalted butter

1 medium shallot (no more than 15 g /½ oz)

2 tsp lemon juice

Put the dulse in a bowl and pour on enough boiling water to barely cover it, when the dulse is pressed down. Heat the butter gently in a frying pan. Chop the shallots extremely finely, add them to the pan and sauté gently until very soft, but not coloured. Pour the dulse and soaking water into the frying pan, add the lemon juice and stir it into the onion. Continue cooking gently, stirring continuously until all the liquid has disappeared and the mixture is smooth and very thick and glossy. Remove from the heat, and transfer to a bowl. Serve warm.

Makes 1 small bowl, to serve 4

Dulse Butter 2

When I was experimenting with dulse butter recipes, I found that this was also a good way of making it – paler in colour, milder and creamier than the richly flavoured warm black butter. Both butters are good. This one is excellent for basting fish as it cooks. Or chill it into a small cylinder shape and cut thin slices to serve on fillets or cutlets.

25 g (1 oz) dulse

1 medium shallot (no more than 15 g /½ oz)

75 g (3 oz) unsalted butter

1½ tsp lemon juice

Follow the previous recipe, but melt only 25 g (1 oz) of the butter in the frying pan to cook the shallot, then adding the soaked dulse and lemon juice. Reduce the mixture to a thick glossy consistency, as above, then remove from the heat and allow to cool. Meanwhile beat the remaining butter in a bowl until very creamy, then beat in the dulse mixture thoroughly. Take a treble thickness of greaseproof paper about 25 x 13 cm (10 x 5") and roll it into a cylinder with a diameter of about 5 cm (2"). Fix with paper clips or sellotape and stand the cylinder in a coffee mug or small jam jar. Spoon the mixture into the greaseproof cylinder, pushing it against the sides to fill out the shape, then refrigerate. When well chilled, unroll the greaseproof paper and take out the cylinder of dulse butter. This can then be neatly sliced into thin circles for melting over fish or vegetables.

Dulse Crisps

These need to be eaten as soon as possible after they have cooled, while they are still really crisp. Try munching them between sips of creamy Irish stout. Kelp (kombu) makes good crisps too.

25 g (1 oz) dried dulse

15-25 g (½-1 oz) butter

Snip the dulse into 1 cm (½") thick strips. Heat the butter in a frying pan. When it is hot (do not let it burn) add the dulse strips and fry them, turning occasionally until they change to a paler colour and start to bubble slightly. Remove, drain on kitchen towel, cool, then serve immediately.

Makes 1 bowl

Carragheen Mould

Carragheen, to my mind, is the prettiest of all the edible seaweed; as you soak the dried tangle it unfolds into swirls of delicate pink and cream laciness – almost too nice to cook.

This recipe is from the Hebrides. The pudding cools to a glossy, finely freckled finish. If you don't like the faint ocean flavour of carragheen, try using almond essence instead of vanilla, but don't judge until you have tasted this version drenched in cream.

10 g (¼ oz) dried carragheen

750 ml (1¼ pt) whole milk

2 - 3 strips lemon peel

1 tsp lemon juice

2 tbs sugar

1 egg yolk

few drops of natural vanilla essence

lemon slices, or a little pinky-purple frond of
    soaked carragheen, to decorate

double cream, to serve

Rinse the dried carragheen under running water, then pick over it before placing it in a bowl of water and leaving it to soak for 15 minutes. Pour the milk into a saucepan. Drain the carragheen, then add it, with the lemon peel to the milk. Bring the milk to the boil, then simmer it for about 30 minutes until the carragheen expands and becomes quite gelatinous and the mixture starts to thicken. Strain the milk into a bowl. Rub the softened carragheen through a fine sieve and return it to the saucepan with the milk. Stir in the sugar, egg yolk, lemon juice and vanilla essence and simmer very gently for a minute or two longer, stirring continuously. Pour the mixture into a wetted mould and leave for about 2½ hours to set. Decorate with lemon slices or a frond of carragheen and serve with slightly sweetened whipped cream.

Variation

Omit the egg yolk and vanilla and add three or four elderflower heads to the simmering milk and carragheen about 5 minutes before straining. You may want to reduce the sugar in this variation.

Serves 4

Irish Moss Ginger Pudding

Citrus rind and root ginger give a tangy flavour to this traditional Irish pudding which is set using carragheen seaweed, or Irish moss. Use water instead of milk if you like a fresher, less creamy taste. Use unwaxed citrus fruits if you can. Alternatively, scrub the fruit thoroughly to remove residues before grating.

Serve with cream and a little stem ginger syrup (or use the recipe below). The variation on this recipe, Irish Moss Pudding with Rich Whiskey Sauce, is my favourite carragheen pudding.

15 g (½ oz) carragheen

900 ml (1½ pt) milk

1 lemon

1 orange

4 cm (1½") piece of root ginger

2-3 tsp sugar

TO DECORATE

1 banana

2 tsp lemon juice

SYRUP

½ tsp grated root ginger

40 g (1½ oz) caster sugar

juice of ½ lemon

7 tbs water

Rinse the carragheen under hot water to remove any salt and grit, then pick over it before placing it in a saucepan with the milk. Finely grate the peel of the lemon and orange and add these to the saucepan. Peel and grate the root ginger and add to the milk. Bring to the boil, then reduce the heat and simmer gently or until the mixture thickens. Stir in the sugar and cook for 1 minute more. Strain the mixture through a fine sieve, then pour it into a wetted mould. Allow it to cool, then chill it in the refrigerator for 3-4 hours.

To make the syrup, put all the ingredients in a small saucepan and boil for about 8 minutes, then strain and cool. Turn the ginger mould out on to a plate and decorate with banana slices dipped in lemon juice. Serve with syrup and cream.

Variation

For Irish Moss Pudding with Rich Whiskey Sauce, leave out the ginger from the above recipe, and serve the pudding with whipped cream and the sauce, which is made by gently simmering the finely grated rind of half a lemon and 50 g (2 oz) soft, dark brown sugar in 150 ml (¼ pt) water for 15 minutes; mashing 2 tsp cornflour into 25 g (1 oz) unsalted butter; gradually stirring the butter mixture into the syrup until it thickens; and removing from the heat and stirring in 1 tbs whiskey. Decorate with orange slices.

Serves 4

Apple Kanten

A traditional Japanese jelly, or kanten, is made from agar. "Kanten" means cold sky in Japanese, so named because the agar gel, after being extracted from the seaweed by boiling, is traditionally left out in the crisp winter air to cool. For 2 weeks the bars of agar are allowed to thaw each day and then freeze at night, until they are completely dry. They are then shaved into tiny flakes, or sold as strands or bars.

Delicate, clean-tasting fruit kanten, served very chilled, makes a refreshing end to a meal – as far removed from children's wobbly birthday jellies as fresh-fruit sorbets are from ice pops. You can use any fruit in season in place of satsumas.

> **450 ml (¾ pt) apple juice**
>
> **2 tbs agar flakes**
>
> **½ unwaxed lemon**
>
> **2 peppermint sprigs (optional)**
>
> **pinch salt**
>
> **4 satsumas**

Put the apple juice in a saucepan. Add the agar flakes. Slice the lemon very thinly, then add it to the saucepan with one peppermint sprig and the salt. Heat, stirring occasionally, until the agar flakes dissolve. Meanwhile peel the satsumas and slice them horizontally across the segments. Arrange the slices in the bottom of an oiled mould. Pour the apple juice mixture slowly through a fine sieve on to the fruit. Rearrange the fruit if it floats out of position. Leave in a cool place to set. Chill, then serve decorated with peppermint leaves.

Serves 4-6

Almond Custard

This simple but beautifully delicate Chinese dessert is made from agar which is widely used for jellies and sweets in the Far East, and which is extracted from various species of seaweed. The dried agar flakes have only the faintest whisper of an ocean flavour which disappears altogether in the finished dessert. Agar sets more easily than gelatine to give a firm but silkily light texture. I use a wetted glass ovenproof dish as a plain square mould when making this recipe.

900 ml (1½ pt) water

2 tbs agar flakes

2 tbs granulated sugar

250 ml (8 fl. oz) evaporated milk

2 drops natural almond essence

DECORATION

dried mango slices, pre-soaked, angelica, natural-coloured glacé cherries, flaked almonds

Bring water to the boil, then sprinkle in the agar. Lower heat and simmer for 5 minutes, stirring until flakes are thoroughly dissolved. Add the sugar and stir till dissolved. Add the evaporated milk and almond essence, stir, then pour into a wetted rectangular mould or shallow tray. Leave to set. When set, cut into six neat rectangles and place on individual plates. Decorate with thin strips of mango, angelica, and glacé cherry, and flaked almonds to make flower shapes. Alternatively, use crystallised fruits.

Serves 6

Apple Snow

Ian Tittley is an expert on seaweed at the Natural History Museum in London. When he gives talks to visiting school children, he often whips up a seaweed-based dish for them to try, and apple snow set with agar is one of them. (Traditional Victorian recipes for apple snow use beaten egg white, but agar and carragheen are useful alternatives if you are reluctant to serve dishes with raw egg these days, and they are suitable for vegetarians.)

Apple snow is a delightful, simple, old-fashioned foamy dessert which makes a light and refreshing end to a substantial meal.

2 tbs water, plus 150 ml (¼ pt)

juice and grated rind of ½ lemon (unwaxed if possible)

1 kg (2 lb) cooking apples

2 tbs agar flakes

125-175 g (4-6 oz) sugar (depending on the sweetness of the apples)

angelica, to decorate

ratafias, to serve

Put the 2 tbs water, lemon juice and rind in a heavy-bottomed pan. Peel, core and slice the cooking apples and add them to the pan, tossing them in the lemon juice and water to prevent them browning as you work. Heat the pan gently and cook the apples on a low heat, stirring regularly, until they form a smooth purée. Put the 150 ml (¼ pt) water in a small saucepan, sprinkle on the agar and heat, stirring, until the agar dissolves. Stir in 125 g (4 oz) sugar and continue heating until it dissolves. Stir the agar mixture into the apple purée. Test for sweetness and add more sugar if the purée is too tart and continue cooking for a moment or two until the extra sugar has dissolved. Stir the mixture thoroughly, then set it aside to cool. As the mixture solidifies and is close to setting, use a balloon whisk to vigorously beat the purée until it is light and frothy. Pour the apple snow into four wine glasses. Chill. Cut 8 matchstick-thin pieces of angelica, and just before serving arrange two in each glass. Serve each with two or three ratafias on the side.

Serves 4

Jamaican Sea Moss

This is a traditional Jamaican drink, a kind of lightly spiced, thickened milk shake. When it is made in Britain, carragheen or Irish moss is used as the thickener, but in the West Indies local species of "sea moss" are used. You can also buy the drink ready-made in cans from West Indian grocers and in Caribbean restaurants. The recipe for this home-made version was given to me by Mr Oates who runs the West Indian grocery stall at Aylesbury market. Traditional versions often also include linseed boiled up with the seaweed. You can add this if you like; it is available from healthfood shops and West Indian grocers.

You can adapt the flavourings in this recipe as you wish, adding vanilla, almond, cinnamon or whatever. In Jamaica, this drink has the reputation of being an aphrodisiac, as well as all-round pick-me-up.

15 g (½ oz) dried carragheen

1.3 litre (2¼ pt) water

1 cinnamon stick

2 tsp linseed (optional)

1 x 400 g (14 oz) can condensed milk

few drops vanilla

a little freshly grated nutmeg

Rinse the carragheen under running water, then put it in a bowl and cover it with water. Leave it to soak for about 10 minutes. Drain the seaweed, pick over it, then place it in a saucepan with the water and cinnamon stick, and linseed if using. Bring to the boil and simmer until it thickens. Strain, discard the seaweed, cinnamon stick and linseed and return the thickened liquid to the pan. Add the condensed milk, vanilla essence and nutmeg to taste. Whisk well, then leave it to cool. As the liquid starts to set, whisk it vigorously. When it is cool, whisk again, then place it in the refrigerator to chill. Whisk again immediately before serving.

Makes about 1 litre (1¾ pt)

Directory of suppliers

Independent healthfood shops are the best places to find dried seaweeds. One of the leading brands you will find is Clearspring. If your local healthfood store does not stock dried seaweed, ask them to get some in – they will probably be able to order it, especially kelp (kombu), laver (nori), dulse, wakame, hijiki and arame. The large healthfood chains may not be so helpful.

FRESH AND DRIED SEAWEED:

The French Garden Ltd
C44 New Covent
Garden Market
0171 498 0277
Sell fresh seaweed and
samphire.

Freshlands
196 Old Street
London EC1V 9FR
0171 490 3170
Sells dried dulse, kelp
(kombu), laver (nori and
sushi nori), wakame,
hijiki, arame;
mail order service.

Seagreens Ltd
Ivor House
21 Ivor Place
Marylebone
London NW1 6EU
0171 723 8899
Fax 0171 723 6131
www.seagreens.com
Harvests fresh, wild
arctic seaweed for a
range of branded
products for cooking
and baking (such as
Seagreens Culinary
Granules and Seagreens
Wild Seaweed Purée),
drinks, nutritional

food capsules and
tablets available direct
and from food stores.

Taste of the Wild
31 London Stone Estate
Broughton Street
London SW8 3QJ
0171 498 5654
fax 0171 498 5419
Fresh seaweeds
including dulse, sea
lettuce, wakami, laver
(nori), kelp (kombu),
samphire. Personal
callers or mail order
(minimum mail order
£20, delivery £10).
All seaweeds except
samphire are packed in
rock salt so they keep
for 2 months in a fridge.

Wild Oats
210 Westbourne Grove
London W11 2RH
0171 229 1063
Sells dried dulse, kelp
(kombu), laver (nori and
sushi nori), wakame,
hijiki, arame; mail order
service.

Oriental grocers:
Chinese grocery shops are
likely to sell dried laver
(nori) and kelp (kombu).
If you are lucky enough to
be near a Japanese food
shop, you will have no
problem getting all kinds
of dried Japanese seaweed.

Supermarkets:
Tesco: sells 100 g punnets
of fresh, rock-salted sea
lettuce and dulse.

J Sainsbury: sells
kombu in 69 stores in
England.

Waitrose: sells nori and
in selected branches they
sell 100 g punnets of
fresh French-harvested
seaweed, called Seaweed
Selection. The varieties
included vary according
to the season. Usually
contain dulse, sea lettuce
and *Haricot de Mer* (Sea
Bean). They will also
shortly be stocking
samphire. Branches
which do not carry stock
can order if requested.

Food Halls:
Harrods
Knightsbridge
London SW1X 7XL
0171 730 1234
Sells toasted dried
laver (sushi nori) and
canned laverbread;
mail order service.

Harvey Nichols
Knightsbridge
London SW1X 7RJ
0171 235 5000
Sells dried laver (nori),
wakame and other
Japanese seaweed;
mail order service.

Howells of Cardiff
S. Glamorgan
01222 231055
Sells canned laverbread;
local delivery service.

Fishmongers:
Check your local
fishmonger for
fresh samphire June-
August; if they don't
have any, they may be
able to get some in.

E. Ashtons
Cardiff Market
01222 229201
Sells fresh laver purée
(laverbread).

Newnes of Billingsgate
Market
0171 515 0793
You will find fresh
samphire in season.

Heritage Fine Foods
of Barrow Gurney
near Bristol
01275 474707
Sells fresh imported
and British samphire in
season, and pickled
samphire as well as
seafood and game;
delivery charge for
orders under £100;
mail order service.

Others: Look out for
fresh laver purée in
Swansea and other
markets in South Wales.
Out of This World
Natural Products in
Clifton, near Bristol also
sells it (0117 946 6897),
as does **Massey's of**
Barnstaple in Devon
(01271 42652) fresh
September-April,
frozen at other times.
mail order service.

Wholesalers and mail
order firms:
Green Seaweeds
Keith Nilson
39 Luton Road
Chatham
Kent ME4 5AG
Sells dried carragheen,
dulse, kelps and other
seaweed when available,
by mail order.

WALES

The Welsh Barrow
PO Box 218
Mumbles
Swansea SA3 4ZA
Supplies canned
laverbread by mail order
enquiries: Presdee-
Hunter Associates
0171 582 5760

IRELAND

Carabay Seaweeds
Kylebroughlan
Moycullen
Co Galway
Ireland
00 35391 85112
Harvests and sells dulse,
carragheen, laver, kelp;
wholesale and by mail
order.

USA

Main Sea Vegetables
Shore Road
Franklin
Maine 04634
USA
207 565 2907
Fax 207 565 2144
Sells organic quality
dried alaria, kelp, dulse
and whole dried laver
plants; wholesale and by
mail order.

Index